Comprehensive Peace Education

Educating for Global Responsibility

Comprehensive Peace Education
Educating for Global Responsibility

Betty A. Reardon

Teachers College, Columbia University
New York and London

Published by Teachers College Press, 1234 Amsterdam Avenue,
New York, NY 10027

Library of Congress Cataloging-in-Publication Data

Reardon, Betty.
  Comprehensive peace education.

  Bibliography: p.
  Includes index.
  1. Peace—Study and teaching.   I. Title.
JX1904.5.R4   1988   327.1′72′07   87-18045

ISBN 0-8077-2886-1
ISBN 0-8077-2885-3 (pbk.)

Manufactured in the United States of America

93 92 91 90 89 88   1 2 3 4 5 6

Contents

Acknowledgments

While any mistakes or misinterpretations are mine alone, this book is the product of learning with and from colleagues and students who share a commitment to making education an instrument of peace. I hope that from among them will come arguments with and additions to these assessments and reflections. To all I extend my thanks for their commitment and their contributions.

I want, too, to convey appreciation for their work on this volume and the companion curriculum collection to Peter Sieger, who carried out the editorial process with care and creativity, and to Gabriella Oldham, who "processed" the words with a watchful and precise eye and with considerable patience.

Thanks also to Linda Farcey, State University of New York at Binghamton, and Mac Freeman, Queens University, Canada, whose lecture invitations provided me with opportunities to first articulate my thoughts on the context and purpose of comprehensive peace education.

Introduction

The reflections offered in this book are for me — as well as for the readers, I hope — only a beginning. The field of peace education is young, vital, and offers many opportunities for the development of new programs, new approaches — indeed, whole new systems of pedagogy that can respond to the most urgent current need of human society: the need for the exercise of global responsibility in the ordering of a just, peaceful, and viable global polity.

This book contains my own, necessarily subjective, reflections on the evolution of peace education and my hopes for its future. It is in no way intended to be a historical overview of the development of the field, though clearly such a history of the movement — the ideas, people, and events that have gone to make it up — is greatly needed. Indeed, since my own understanding of the field has changed considerably over the years, these reflections are as much an account of my own development as a peace educator as of my experience with the field.

I became involved in writing this book as a direct outcome of my participation in a project initiated by the World Policy Institute, undertaken in cooperation with the former director of the institute's Academic Outreach Program, Barbara Wien. Barbara and I had agreed that in addition to the need for a resource that made peace education materials readily accessible to classroom teachers (which we have addressed in the companion to this volume, *Educating for Global Responsibility: Teacher-Designed Curricula for Peace Education, K–12* [New York: Teachers College Press, 1988]), there was also a need to begin to define the field: to help educators and citizens alike understand the need for peace education, what constitutes peace education, and how it is and should be pursued. It seemed to us that our project might make a significant contribution toward that definitional task. As I began to prepare the curriculum guide by reviewing the materials we had gathered in our survey of teacher-designed curricula, however, it soon became clear that not only did the word *peace* bear many definitions and connotations, but *peace education* itself meant many different things, even to those who identified themselves as peace educators. I also felt that it would be both presumptuous and premature to specifically define and delimit a field that is, I believe, only at the beginning stage of what it might become. However, it was clear that for the purposes of my own work and that of at least those of my colleagues in the field with whom I have shared some of these reflections, it was time to become much more self-conscious about both the pedagogical purposes and the political goals of peace education. We need to go beyond the immediate aim of preparing for nonviolent politics and investigate the root causes of the violent conditions we face so that we can determine how education can be used to interrupt the cycle of ever-increasing violence in which we are now swept up. This book is my effort to begin this task.

Stated most succinctly, the general purpose of peace education, as I understand it, is to promote the development of an authentic planetary consciousness that will enable us to function as global citizens and to transform the present human condition by changing the social structures and the patterns of thought that have created it. This transformational imperative must, in my view, be at the center of peace education.

It is important to emphasize that *transformation*, in this context, means a profound, global, cultural change that affects ways of thinking, world views, values, behaviors, relationships, and the structures that make up our public order. It implies a change in the human consciousness and in human society of a dimension far greater than any other that has taken place since the emergence of the nation-state system, and perhaps since the emergence of human settlements. Obviously this is no small task, and certainly no curriculum development can be anything more than the most minor element of such a process. Indeed, the comprehensive form of peace education that I advocate can, even in its broadest dimensions, make only a limited contribution to the transformational learning process that is now under way, part of a complex pattern of trends moving us toward the true humanization of the human species. Opposing these positive developments are countertrends of greater violence, factionalism, alienation, and degradation of all life forms. The challenge to education is to transform itself into an instrument that can synergize all of the elements of the positive trend so as to transcend the latter.

It is only fairly recently that I have begun to glimpse the nature of this potential transformation. My own experience, I think, is similar to that of others who have worked in peace education for a number of years. Our perceptions and, therefore, our professional practices have gone through three phases. The approaches characteristic of each of these phases still exist, in various forms, in peace education today. Each approach is, to some extent, still part of my own work. All three are woven throughout these reflections. It is not my intent to say that one is better than another in terms of its intellectual content or teaching methodology. Each, I would argue, has some place in a comprehensive approach. But because each succeeding phase used a wider and deeper approach than the preceding one, the three must be distinguished here, both to provide a developmental background for my discussion of the current and future directions of the field and to define some basic terminology.

The three phases that have comprised this development are (in chronological order) the *reform* phase, dating from the end of World War II, the *reconstructive* phase, developed in the 1960s, and the *transformational* phase, currently evolving. The approach used in each phase is characterized by certain assumptions about the causes of war and about how education could help to create the conditions needed for peace. Each approach embraces a different political goal, and therefore each pursues a somewhat different set of pedagogical objectives.

The goal of the *reform approach* is to prevent war. It focuses on the prevention of war and the control of arms races. The changes sought toward that end, including those required for intermediate objectives, are all changes in behaviors: of people — particularly people as citizens — and of nations. The central thesis is that if people and nations behaved differently, gave more consideration to nonviolent alternatives, war could be prevented.

The *reconstructive approach* reaches beyond these behavioral objectives, seeking to reconstruct international systems, to abolish war, and to achieve total disarmament. Its objective, therefore, is primarily structural and institutional, rather than behavioral, change. Reconstructive teaching centers on ways of changing institutions and explores the notion of establishing global institutions to resolve conflicts and keep the peace.

The *transformational approach* seeks a larger, more comprehensive goal: the rejection of all violence, not just arms races and war. The goal of the transformational approach is to make violence unacceptable, not only in interactions among individuals but also in interactions among nations, and to make violent consequences unacceptable in foreign-policy planning. The changes sought are behavioral and institutional but also, and primarily, changes in thinking and in the formation of values. It is the transformational approach that, in my view, holds the most promise for the future of peace education.

One of the common elements that runs through all of the approaches is the emphasis on value questions — a major reason why the field of peace education has been so controversial. The reform approach, for example, challenges the way in which social values are applied, especially in the formulation of public policy. The reconstructive approach challenges not only the application of the values but the processes by which values are derived and the way in which policies are made—the systems themselves. The transformational approach takes this one step further, for in addition to questioning the ways in which values are applied, and the institutional values of the present system, it also challenges some of the fundamental value assumptions and the very bases of the social order.

The three approaches lend themselves to different kinds of pedagogical modes. The reform and reconstructive approaches generally employ an instructive mode. The notion is that we need to inform: to provide certain information and to develop certain skills that will enable people to engage in the particular critical processes needed for reform and reconstruction. In the transformational approach, the emphasis is more on an educative mode in the sense of "drawing out," or eliciting, learning. It is this educative mode that I hope will become the pedagogical focus of peace education as we seek to build a comprehensive approach directed toward transformation. This has, it seems, been what many of us have been striving for in the development of a pedagogy of peace—effective learning for global responsibility.

Comprehensive peace education, to me, connotes peace education that takes place at every level, and in every subject area, of formal education. Formal education, however, is only one component of the total educative process needed to achieve authentic peace. Although in most of this book I will be concerned primarily with formal education, especially the education of teachers and of secondary and elementary school students, the general principles discussed here can and should operate in all of the spheres of intentional learning that we call education—both formal and informal—and throughout life. Indeed, I propose an education that is integral, or essential, to each stage of life and phase of experience, a developmental education based on the assumption of constant change and on the understanding that different kinds of knowledge are needed at different stages of life and in various cultures and geopolitical environments. Yet some common principles and values should operate throughout all realms of human education and in all cycles of learning. I have tried to outline some of these as they relate to comprehensive peace education for teachers and students. Comprehensive peace education, then, also means *global* education, in the sense that it comprehends all that is relevant, but also in the sense that it relates to all human interactions on Planet Earth and to human interactions with the Earth.

In this book I am primarily concerned with what I refer to as *peace education*, rather than *peace studies*. Peace education I see as distinct from peace studies because of its emphasis on the learning process. *Peace studies*, the more comprehensive term, connotes to me the process of acquiring specific knowledge—largely, but not entirely, through peace research (as I discuss in Chapter 4). Because peace studies belongs mainly to the academic realm, the terms *peace education* and *peace studies* often are taken to indicate the differentiation between elementary and secondary endeavors and those at the college level. However, in this book I am less concerned with the level of formal education at which they are practiced than with the emphasis that each brings to the educational task, one being on the learning process termed *education*, the other being on the acquisition and command of knowledge termed *studies*. Both are important, but I am concerned more with how we can facilitate the learning process, which is, I believe, essential to the application of the knowledge.

A few other terms are also important throughout this book. The knowledge base for curriculum development for both peace education and peace studies, as I have indicated, is primarily the product of *peace research*, the third area of the formal academic field. Peace research is becoming a discipline and as such provides the basis for those academic programs that are called peace studies. All three of these areas, however, are but a small part of the total *peace learning movement*, which, in turn, is but a component of the general *transformational learning movement* that I referred to earlier as taking place throughout the world today. *Peace action*, or what some refer to as *peace development* — specific endeavors to carry out peace learning and apply peace knowledge in the public realm — is both a product and a component of the larger peace learning process. It too is mainly reformist and reconstructive, but for many of its practitioners the ultimate purpose is to prepare for effective action toward transformation.

I should like to see comprehensive peace education become the mediator and interpreter of developments in all three realms — research, study, and action. I hope that this book will encourage others to make their own interpretations, to experiment with ways of preparing students for peace action, and to enter into a discourse on what should constitute that preparation and how our experiences to date can be used to provide the basis for a truly comprehensive approach to peace education. The field is at a significant point of transition. I urge others who feel the same intense need for collaboration and exchange among peace educators that I do to join in as we work to build on the highly promising beginnings and to develop comprehensive peace education as the core of all elementary and secondary education.

CHAPTER 1

Personal Perspectives and General Approaches

Since the reflections that follow are admittedly idiosyncratic and personal, it may help the reader to interpret them if I sketch the particular influences that have affected my philosophy of peace education. As I review my own development as a peace educator, I am aware of four major influences that formed the definitions and directions that I offer in this book: world order inquiry, transnational cooperation, national networking, and feminist studies.

World Order Studies: A Mode of Inquiry

The Institute for World Order, an organization established to conduct peace research and education, began its work in the field of secondary education in 1963 with the initiation of its high school program. I left my position as a social studies teacher in a secondary school to direct the program. The assumptions that gave rise to that program were, first, that the civic education offered in secondary schools was the most promising arena for the introduction of the serious study of peace issues to the broadest possible sector of the American public and, second, that the major cause of war was the lack of adequate international peacekeeping and dispute-settlement procedures. The educational task was to introduce to the American public alternatives to war, in the form of possibilities for new international institutions. The initial efforts, therefore, focused on materials development and on preparing teachers to offer instruction about peacekeeping and dispute settlement. The approach developed over the first five years of the program was based on the assertion that study of the issues must take place within a context that was global, interdisciplinary, based on a systems approach to the study of peacekeeping and dispute-settlement procedures, futuristic, and value-based.

All but the focus on peacekeeping and the value base became characteristic of the mainstream "international education" of the 1960s, the forerunner of "global education" (definitions of these two fields follow in chapters 2 and 3). The issue of values tended to separate the emerging field of world order studies from the fields of international relations and international education. The openly acknowledged value base of world order studies was often cited as evidence that it was advocacy rather than inquiry, propaganda rather than scholarship. Although many gifted scholars were involved in world order studies, their efforts were deemed marginal to the social sciences they practiced. This marginalization seemed to push the field ever deeper into a questioning of structures and prevailing values and even of the basic assumptions of the disciplines, giving it a reputation of belonging to the radical wing of international studies—a position that members of the field themselves acknowledged in specifying the characteristics that distinguished it from the mainstream. Some years later, the then director of the institute's Transnational Academic Program, Burns Weston, outlined the distinctions:

> Preliminarily, it needs emphasizing that an optimal human survival curriculum, or what I choose to call "world order education," would be at once innovative and traditional in its approach to internationally oriented instruction. It would be innovative because it would emphasize global perspectives, interdisciplinary analyses, and futuristic thinking, and it would be traditional because, in total keeping with "the compleat liberal education," it would be centrally concerned with the meaning, value, and improvement of life *as a whole*. . . . [Figure 1], contrasting . . . "traditional" and "world order" approaches to the study of international affairs, quickly illustrates what would be principally involved. Also, because it would presuppose a basic although perhaps unjustified optimism that solutions to the grave conditions which presently threaten human survival are within human capability, a human survival or world order curriculum would be as much concerned with how as with what one teaches and learns (Weston et al., 1978, pp. 7–8).

Weston's description of world order studies was a pedagogical version of the peace research and concepts resulting from the institute's World Order Models Project (WOMP), carried on by a kind of multinational traveling think tank of scholars from all parts of the world, who met regularly to collaborate on common research efforts. WOMP was initiated in 1970 because, the initiators asserted, the imperative of a global perspective on such studies called for cross-national endeavors to assure that the problems under study were viewed from a variety of cultural and ideological perspectives. Contrary to the popular notion that the global approach simply constituted a consideration of the entire "in-

Figure 1. Approaches to the Study of International Affairs

Traditional Approaches	*World Order Approach*
1. Analysis is presumed value free	1. Analysis is value-oriented – aimed at value clarification and realization
2. Ultimate analytical goal is description	2. Ultimate analytical goal is prescription
3. Time dimension is past and present	3. Time dimension is past, present and especially future
4. Problems seen as separate issues	4. Problems seen as interrelated issues
5. Focuses on nation-states and governmental elites	5. Focuses on range of actors, from individuals to supranational institutions
6. Policy goals defined in terms of national interests	6. Policy goals defined in terms of global interests
7. Power seen as basically military and economic manipulation	7. Power seen as not only the ability to coerce
8. Large-scale violence considered an acceptable means to implement policy goals	8. Large-scale violence ordinarily considered unacceptable
9. Human survival assumed	9. Human survival deemed problematical

Source: Weston et al., 1978, pp. 7–8.

ternational" system, for WOMP the term *global* meant to view problems from the perspective of the entire planet and the whole of humanity.

The scholars associated with WOMP also made significant distinctions between the terms *international* and *transnational*, using the former for matters involving governments and the latter for nongovernmental matters that transcend national boundaries. This distinction has become quite important, now that peace movements involve people from many nations, who often oppose the policies of their own national governments. It is extremely important, too, to the rapidly developing concept of global citizenship, so central to the purposes of peace education. WOMP itself is a model of transnational efforts by scholars who are exercising the responsibilities of global citizenship, acting to enhance the interests of the world as a single community.

The WOMP study also led to the identification of a broader range of problems to be studied in considering the issues of war and peace. The intersection of the value base and the transnational perspectives gave the field a substantive base that went beyond the initial concern with armed conflict and made it quite clear that global and transnational perspectives are distinct from both the national and the international points of view. As a result of WOMP, *world order studies* came to comprise an inquiry into the solution of five problems, defined in terms of five *world order values*. This schema became the foundation for curriculum development at the university and secondary levels, and the approach began to be discussed in the professional literature. In my own contribution to the 1973 yearbook of the Association for Supervision and Curriculum Development, I outlined the world order approach as follows:

> World order seeks not only nonviolent solutions to conflicts but, even more important, *just* solutions to conflicts. It is a normative, value-centered discipline which aspires to more than the elimination of war, aiming also at relieving human suffering resulting from the drastically disparate distribution of the world's wealth; from the prejudices, discrimination, and oppression which deprive far too many human beings of their rights and dignity; and from the wanton exploitation of the earth's resources by that powerful minority which controls and uses them without regard to the interests of people of this and succeeding generations. The search for just solutions is expressed by world order as an attempt to achieve five goals:
>
> 1. The minimization of violence, or *war prevention*
> 2. The maximizing of *economic welfare*, or the providing of better standards of living for more people
> 3. The increasing of *social justice* by relieving discrimination and oppression
> 4. The broadening of the democratic base of public policy making by increasing the *participation* of minorities and individuals in decision-making processes
> 5. The improving of the quality of life through restoration of *ecological balance*
>
> World order examines these goals by asking some significant questions: What is the present state of the world with regard to peace, economic welfare, social justice, political participation, and ecological balance? If we make no significant changes in the international system, what is the state likely to be in the next generation? If that state is, as most trend analyses indicate, not one likely to achieve peace and the other related world-order goals, what changes in the system would be most likely to do so? How can we bring about those changes? (The individual components of the inquiry described below are italicized.)

The methodology of world order encompasses many techniques of inquiry and active learning which offer some hope for improving education on values and public issues. There are five basic steps to this methodology. The first is the *diagnosis*: a summary and analysis of the world problems, their causes and their relationship to the . . . values. The second step is a *prognosis* or a projection of the evolution of these problems and the potential for the emergence of other problems over a twenty- to thirty-year period. These two are preliminary to a third step which actually attempts to deal with the future in the *positing of several alternative international systems* designed to resolve the problems defined in the first step. This projection is followed by the *evaluation* of the alternatives and selection of a *preferred system* — the alternative which emerges from the evaluation as the one most likely to achieve peace, economic welfare, and social justice in the world community. The final step, *transition*, plots the strategies and policies needed to transform the present world system into the "preferred world." (Reardon, 1973, pp. 133–134)

My interest in the developments emerging from WOMP and my use of the world order approach in my own work with teacher education and curriculum development gave me the framework within which I still tend to view global issues and provided a systematic mode of inquiry into the causes of war and conditions of peace that I still find useful. Although I came to be a severe critic of what seemed to me its biases (Reardon, 1985), the world order approach has served me and other peace educators well as a substantive foundation (and, it should be noted, the approach has continued to develop and mature).

The Peace Education Commission: Transnational Efforts

During the years in which WOMP was conducting its initial research, a group of educators belonging to the International Peace Research Association (IPRA) formed an active transnational network, the Peace Education Commission (originally founded as the Peace Education Committee at IPRA's 1972 biennial meeting in Bled, Yugoslavia). The Peace Education Commission (PEC), consisting of members from all regions of the world, began its work at a crucial time in the history of peace research. Most of the members of the association had been researching issues related to arms races and international conflict as major causes of war. But much as WOMP's transnationalism had transformed the substance of world order studies, so too the emerging issues concerning the developing world drastically changed the parameters of peace research, and consequently of peace education. The issues of underdevelopment, poverty, militarism, and repression produced new approaches and concepts, many of which are now widely incorporated into peace education curricula throughout the world. Although as yet the data and concepts produced by peace research have not been widely incorporated into American practice, they have had profound effects on theories of peace education, especially in Europe.

As a consequence of these conceptual developments, two new approaches — *development education* and *human rights education* — were integrated into peace education, starting in Europe in the late 1960s and in the United States somewhat later. Development education, which has as its critical concern world poverty and underdevelopment, focused primarily on the economic relations between the industrial nations and the developing ones. Human rights education centered on international human rights standards and their constant and widespread violation. With these approaches came an intense interest in the pedagogical theories of dialogue and consciousness-raising, associated with Paolo Freire (1973). These two areas of human rights and development, considered integral to the field as a whole, also came to be viewed as interrelated, interdependent issues and fields equally important to peace, much as world order studies views its five central value concerns as integrally related (Marks, 1983).

The focus on the dialogic method was but one manifestation of an interest in participatory approaches to learning and an indicator of peace educators' attraction to critiques of traditional education. The schools and pedagogy were seen as being as much in need of reform as the international system. A decidedly reconstructionist theme began to appear in peace education discourse.

The work of members of the Peace Education Commission, published mainly in international journals such as the *Bulletin of Peace Proposals* (see Appendix, "Significant Works in the Development of the Pedagogy of Peace"), reflects these developments. Most notable among the influential concepts discussed there are those expressed in the terms *negative peace, positive peace*, and *structural violence* (Galtung, 1968). *Negative peace* became the term for the conceptual category encompassing research and education about wars, arms races, and violent conflicts. The state of negative peace was defined as the absence of war, achieved by the prevention and/or the general reduction and eventual elimination of armed conflict. *Positive peace* encompassed concerns similar to those of development education: the reduction or elimination of poverty, disease, illiteracy, marginalization, and other conditions that lower the economic and material quality of life for the poor and oppressed of the world. Positive peace also included many of the same concerns as human rights education, especially the realization of the full range of human rights — civil and political, as well as economic, cultural, and social. *Structural violence* was the term used to identify the consequences of social, political, and economic structures, institutions, and processes that systematically violate rights and lower the material quality of life of particular groups or classes of people — the same structures that maintain (and are maintained by) the attitudes and values inherent in racism, sexism, and colonialism (Reardon, 1976).

The members of PEC worked together much as the members of the WOMP project had, except that their meetings were always held during conferences called by WOMP, UNESCO, or other international organizations (or transnational agencies). The cross-cultural dialogues and collaboration produced a common diagnosis of the programs that peace education sought to address (see IPRA newsletters, 1976, cited in the Appendix). Yet the approaches and priorities remained varied, rooted in the cultural realities in which the respective educators worked. Differences, even controversies, emerged, but common purposes were able to sustain the diversity. Working closely, in a context of solidarity and friendship, with educators from Europe (Eastern and Western), Africa, Asia, and Latin America has given me a profound belief in the possibility of a multicultural, humane, global community. And if anything has given me an operative global perspective, it has been my participation in PEC.

The Peace Education Network: American Efforts

The Consortium on Peace Research Education and Development, established by university researchers and educators as a North American affiliate of IPRA, also attracted schoolteachers interested in peace education. The Peace Education Network (PEN) was formed in the early seventies as a mechanism through which elementary and secondary school peace educators in the United States could share and enrich their respective efforts, work toward defining and systematizing the young field, and encourage its introduction into the schools. It was one of the most active and productive networks of the entire consortium founded in the late sixties. The network was primarily comprised of educators who were more concerned with issues of justice and conflict than with the structural and theoretical issues on which PEC focused. PEN was largely responsible for introducing and developing nonviolent conflict resolution as a central concept of American peace education. The network's concerns were reflected in its first publication, *A Repertoire of Peacemaking Skills* (Carpenter, 1977). This and other curricular materials designed by PEN members are described in the curriculum guide developed as a companion to this volume (Reardon, 1988).

The curricula developed by PEN emphasized participatory learning, egalitarian classrooms, and inquiry and problem solving rather than didactic methods. These methods derived from applying to education the values of universal human dignity and social justice that were core values to PEN, providing criteria by which to diagnose problems and devise solutions.

Such methods also reflected developments described in the late sixties and the seventies as the "new social studies." Open inquiry into controversial issues; values clarification; simulations, games, and role plays; significant student participation in all phases of planning of the educational process, from selection of content through the evaluation of learning—these were some of the innovations finding their way into social education. Peace educators found these methods to be consistent with their educational values and assessed them as effective instruments for the achievement of their learning goals. They are still among the methods that are assessed in the curriculum guide as the best of peace education (Reardon, 1988).

What I wish most to emphasize about PEN is the concern with justice and nonviolence that so strongly informed its work, in both style and substance. The spirit of PEN was like that of PEC, seeking not only to develop education about injustice and training in nonviolent conflict resolution but also to promote global solidarity. Although not all PEN members had extensive transnational experience, study and human sensitivity gave the group a strong sense of the structural violence in the world and of the need for peace education to make North Americans more aware of their roles in those structures.

Another significant influence on the work of PEN was the role that religion began to play in articulating the ethical and moral dimensions of problems of global peace and justice. Beginning with the publication of "Pacem-in-Terris," the 1963 papal encyclical outlining the stance of the Roman Catholic Church on major problems of world order, Catholic educators (a number of whom have always been active in PEN) took a leadership role in curriculum development and program design. Other churches made similar statements, with special reference to the arms race, and these became sources from which educators could gain more insight into the deeper ethical dimensions of the value issues raised by peace education. Indeed, my own insights into the values and the meaning involved in peacemaking have been considerably deepened by my work with the churches in United Ministries in Education (UME). UME's Peacemaking in Education Program has been built on Christian values, ecumenism, and global solidarity, the elements that have characterized the Christian peace movement, and which the World Council of Churches refers to as "ecumenical learning."

Such values education, however, like much of peace education, was pushed aside with the more conservative political trends of the seventies. Recently, both values education and peace education have been criticized as indoctrination by many in such educational bastions as the American Federation of Teachers and the U.S. Department of Education. For a variety of reasons, which I have discussed elsewhere (Reardon, 1982), peace was not a popular curricular topic. Indeed, for most of the twenty years of the development of peace education described here, the field remained marginal to school curricula, even in courses in international and global education. However, between 1980 and 1982, with the reemergence of a strong and popular nuclear disarmament movement, largely dormant since the sixties, the situation changed dramatically, producing a broad-scale movement among teachers to introduce questions related to arms races and peace into the schools. These more recent efforts (discussed in further detail in Chapter 6), however, have not been significantly influenced by the developments within peace education reviewed here. In many ways it is a new movement, with even greater vigor, and certainly greater numbers, than in the days when PEN was the "only game" in American peace education. It should be kept in mind that in this book I have separated peace education from the larger and related field of global education. The fortunes and the purposes of both have run along parallel, often intertwined paths. The practitioners of both fields have shared resources as well as problems and obstacles. However, here the focus is on peace education, because of its particular substance and concerns, and because my own experience has been in this field.

PEN has given me hope that American education can become a major influence in developing a new global consciousness and the sense of human solidarity that are the two main forces for peace in the world, and that American peace educators can develop a comprehensive approach to peace education capable of synergizing those forces into a transformational learning mode.

The Feminist Movement: Human Efforts

One more perspective has come to my own consciousness more recently, yet its elements have, I think, been at work right along. Most peace education is humanistic, and much of it claims to have as its goal transformation of the human condition. My conscious experience of both emphases, however, has come from my work in feminist approaches to peace research, which I have described elsewhere (Reardon, 1983, 1984, 1985). Most of the elements of what I now define as transformational peace education came into focus for me when I brought a feminist perspective to them. I am sure readers will be able to identify the feminist perspectives throughout this work and see them most vividly expressed in my reflections on context, in Chapter 4, and on purposes in Chapter 5. It is through feminism that I have gained my insights into wholeness and integrity. Feminism is, I believe, the most fully human current perspective on peace and peace education.

CHAPTER 2

Education for Negative Peace

A basic assumption of this book is, as I have said, that practitioners of peace education must begin to define and delimit the field: We need to reach some general agreement on its central concepts, educational goals, and preferred instructional approaches. The intent here is not to impose restricted boundaries to the subject matter, nor to issue "definitive" descriptions of the field, its concepts and its methods. Rather, I hope that a systematic discourse about definitions will lead us to a broader but clearer notion of authentic purposes and methods and the conceptual tools needed to refine them. The definitional problem seems to be one of achieving conceptual clarity without closing off a continued open inquiry into what constitutes peace, how it can be achieved, and how we can educate students to work for it and to live in it as the normal state of human society. In this chapter and the next I offer my own review and assessment of current practices and trends as a step toward the opening of such a discourse.

Peace education, as it is now practiced, appears to me to reflect two trends, one rooted in the developments described in Chapter 1, and the other blossoming from the more recent branches of the field. Both trends can be viewed within the conceptual parameters defined by peace researchers as negative and positive peace, the major domains of their research field. It should be noted that although these are generally accepted as the major conceptual categories of the field, there are some peace researchers who reject this distinction, particularly those who do not regard justice as an essential requirement for peace. A leading opponent of this specific formulation of negative and positive peace is Kenneth Boulding, probably the most distinguished "father" of American peace research. Boulding's concerns lie mainly in the reduction and elimination of warfare.

> Peace is a word of so many meanings that one hesitates to use it for fear of being misunderstood. When, for instance, a group of us started the Center for Research on Conflict Resolution at the University of Michigan in 1956, we conceived it as a center for peace research, but we

deliberately avoided the use of the word "peace" in the title because of the misunderstandings which might arise. The concept of peace has both positive and negative aspects. On the positive side, peace signifies a condition of good management, orderly resolution of conflict, harmony associated with mature relationships, gentleness, and love. On the negative side, it is conceived as the absence of something — the absence of turmoil, tension, conflict, and war.

. . . On the other hand, there is a high valuation of the positive concept of peace, which is seen as a skill in the management of conflict and the development of a larger order than that which involves warring parties. The opposite of this kind of peace is then seen as a clearly pathological state of some kind of war. War or "not-peace" involves the inability to manage conflict, to the cost of both parties. It involves disruptive dialectic, unnecessary confusion, childish quarreling, immaturity of political form. Peace in this larger, more positive sense is quite consistent with conflict and excitement, debate and dialogue, drama and confrontation. But it provides a setting within which these processes do not get out of hand, become pathological, and cause more trouble than they are worth. In this sense of the word, peace is one of the ultimate time's arrows in the evolutionary process, an increasing product of human development and learning. (K. Boulding, 1978, pp. 3, 5)

To Boulding, the first priority for peace research is knowledge that will illuminate, enhance, and extend this "larger order" within a condition that he calls "stable peace," which, as is evident from the passage quoted, he does not consider to be a negative condition.

Researchers such as Galtung, on the other hand, assert that the major tasks lie in uncovering the roots of armed conflict, which, they believe, can frequently be found in conditions of "structural violence" that are not classifiable as war (Galtung, 1969). They see the need to develop knowledge from which the conditions of positive peace can be devised through overcoming various forms of institutional violence. This position is also held by most Christian churches (McIntyre et al., 1976).

As I hope I have made clear already, my own view is that the two concepts are complementary and inseparable. Like Boulding, I see what has been labeled "negative peace" as a desirable and, in many ways, positive condition. His notion of "stable peace" I would term fundamental or *foundational peace*, out of which might grow those conditions of justice and equity connoted by positive peace, which, as a living, evolving condition, I would call *organic peace*. However, for the sake of clarity, throughout this book I will use the terms *negative* and *positive* as they are employed in the wider field of peace research. Peace education practices derive primarily from the concepts of peace held by the practitioners. Most of the concepts used in peace education today fall within the domain of negative peace, but a significant set of concepts within the domain of positive peace is also reflected in contemporary peace education.

Concepts of Negative Peace: Emphasis on Arms Races, War, and Violent Conflict

Peace is problematic not only as a goal but even as a concept. Popular wisdom has often held that peace is unachievable because it is indefinable. Researchers are only the most recent in a long line of would-be definers of peace. Concepts of what constitutes a peaceful society have been suggested by religious scripture and popular prophets, as well as by researchers' "models of world order." Popular images of peace tend to be lyrical rather than concrete. Visions articulated by popular leaders are usually more inspirational than practical, and most models of peace are expressed in scholarly or religious media that have little political currency. People or projects seriously addressing the task of defining and describing a peaceful social order are categorized as utopian (usually in the pejorative sense), even by some fellow members of the peace movement, who, considering themselves to be of a more pragmatic bent, attend mainly to current realities and to immediate possibilities for action on some specific objective in the politics of arms races or international conflicts. Yet without images, concepts cannot take form. Without utopian visions to articulate the conditions of a less violent, more just world, peace cannot be described, and we will continue to lack the basic tools with which to define it. Thus the task of envisioning peace remains a challenge to both the movement and the field of education. Although this task appears to belong primarily to the domain of positive peace, the educational establishment has tended to focus on questions of negative peace, and so the most detailed models of peacekeeping systems that we have also fall within the domain of negative peace. Yet here too there is a real need for images of the possible that go beyond the present limited and fragmented efforts that have viewed peacekeeping as a function distinct from other aspects of the conditions of negative peace. This kind of thinking, as I will note later, is in itself an obstacle to peace.

Some peace education now deals with positive peace, but for many reasons that domain is not so readily defined as negative peace and is not conceptually clear enough for curriculum-planning purposes. We seem to know far more about what is not peace than about what is. Nor has positive peace, long a central concern of the older peace education movement, been the primary focus of the recent upsurge in peace education

exemplified by the establishment of such organizations as United Cam-
puses Against Nuclear War, Educators for Social Responsibility, and Physicians for Social Responsibility. Most recent teaching has focused on
negative peace — that is, on reducing the likelihood of war. It has emphasized the problems posed by arms races and specific cases of international
conflict, and it falls within what I classify as the reform approach to
peace education. However, although the wider emphasis is on negative
peace and the focus is on the problem of armed conflict, the subject of
study is not so much *war* as *wars*. Most current peace education does not
address war as an institution, nor the deepest sociopsychological and
political causes of war that recent feminist approaches to peace research
have asserted as the fundamental problems (Eisler & Loye, 1986). Rather
it deals mainly with single issues and particular cases (such as the proposed nuclear arms freeze or the war in Nicaragua), with the aim of
avoiding or limiting war. In the minds of some peace educators, this
failure to focus on war as an institution or on the "war system" helps to
perpetuate the notion that war itself is too great a problem to tackle.
Thus peace is treated as the absence, avoidance, ending, or limitation of
particular wars (such as those in Central America or Afghanistan) or
between particular parties (such as the United States and the Soviet
Union). In this concentration on negative peace, there is little evidence of
any abolitionist element in current peace education practice. Although
many in the peace movement have embraced the abolition of war as their
goal, the notion that even negative peace could mean the end of war as an
accepted human institution is neither popular among educators nor familiar to students and the public. (Some attempt to introduce the public
to the concept of abolition is, however, currently being made by the
Beyond War movement.) This situation, I believe, is in some measure due
to the lack of visions, images, and holistic models of peace.

Peace in the most global sense, in current American educational
practice, appears mainly to mean an accommodation between the United
States and the Soviet Union. Concord between the superpowers would
certainly contribute to peace, in two ways. It would greatly reduce the risk
of nuclear war, and it would defuse many of the regional hostilities
throughout the world that are heightened by the superpower competition.
If the two powers cease intervening in regional conflicts, such disputes
would be more readily resolved, ended sooner, or even avoided. Peace, in
this context, also means nonintervention by one nation in the affairs of
another.

The notions of nonintervention and the rejection of military means
of dealing with international conflict relate to the concept of peace as
nonviolent conflict resolution. Peace is maintained when conflicts can be

resolved without violence. (Note that both of these concepts are negative, based on the elimination of active armed conflict.) Focus on conflict also places attention on perceptions of competitors and images of the enemy. This focus leads to a concept of peace as tolerance, knowledge, and understanding of others, which, in its broadest sense, would include all the world's peoples. Peace in this sense means international understanding. Greater understanding, it is assumed, would help to avoid war by reducing conflict.

For many peace educators, particularly those using a Christian perspective, peace as an end or a goal is not the main focus. Their emphasis is more on the struggle for peace and the progress of achieving it, so that the notions of "peacekeeping" and "peacemaking" take priority over the prevention of war. With this emphasis they join those peace educators who, perceiving the central problem as the way conflict is handled, base their efforts on teaching *conflict management* and/or *conflict resolution*. Conflict studies, though related to peace education, are in a number of ways a distinct field from either peace education or peace studies. However, many programs, particularly at the university level, combine the two under the title of "peace and conflict studies," emphasizing both the distinction and the relationship between the two fields, and usually focusing on negative peace.

Conflict studies may well be a more rapidly developing field than peace studies. Conflict studies examine all kinds of conflicts and disputes, at all levels of social organization. Indeed, only a small segment of the field focuses on war. Conflict studies treat (among other things) interpersonal conflicts, labor disputes, community conflicts, and international disputes that may or may not lead to war. Courses in negotiation and dispute settlement have become quite popular lately, because of the conflictual and litigious nature of our society, as well as because of our preoccupation with the superpower conflict. Because conflict-management or conflict-resolution skills are seen as essential to most social relations and interactions, they are being introduced into the curriculum of formal education at all levels. Skills for nonviolent conflict resolution, it is believed, may be as necessary to family life as they are to world society. Yet nonviolence and conflict resolution, although gaining ground, are still no more standard as subjects in our curricula than they are as phenomena in our society.

The study of nonviolence, although distinct from the study of negative peace, is related to it when the focus is on conflict resolution, rather than on the philosophy of nonviolence. Its current practitioners, however, seem more involved in the development of notions of positive peace. The notion of peace as the absence of war is comprehended by the concept of nonviolence, in its rejection of the use of force and aggression as tools for achieving political goals or for resisting the goals of others. However, to those who embrace nonviolence philosophically as a belief system, as well as strategically as an approach to conflict resolution, peace is something much broader than the absence of war. Within this context, peace is the absence of violence in all its forms — physical, social, psychological, and structural. Even those who are interested in nonviolence primarily as the most appropriate form of struggle for a just cause (see Gene Sharp's comprehensive accounts of such cases [1974]) have concerns that go beyond international warfare. Historically, nonviolence as a strategy has been and is most widely used in cases of civil strife and local conflict, and these cases have been the main subject of study in the practice of nonviolence.

Both conflict resolution and nonviolence, when used as conceptual bases for education in the realm of negative peace, have as a major objective the development of particular skills — skills that have been honed and tested in numerous practical experiences in the struggle for peace, in the spirit of Gandhi's admonition, "There is no way to peace. Peace is the way." These are skills that I regard as essential to the practice of citizenship in a conflictual nuclear age.

Educational Assumptions and Approaches

Approaches to education about and for the achievement of negative peace derive largely from such concepts of peace as I have just described and from the assumptions about the causes of war that underlie them. The issue of the causes of war is an area in which there are also some significant differences and lively debates among peace educators and peace researchers, and about which there is considerable ignorance among the American public. For the most part, current American practice in peace education, particularly at the elementary and secondary level, neither asserts nor assumes the structural or economic causes of war that are emphasized in peace education in other countries. Even at the university level, little attention is paid to the possibility of psychosocial causes. The most widely evident assumptions about the causes of war reflected in current peace education curricula, which generally take a reformist approach, appear to fall into four categories: (1) political/ideological conflict; (2) arms races; (3) lack of understanding or misperceptions of others; and (4) inadequate use of alternative conflict-resolution procedures. Although all of these factors should be included in a study of causes, none is adequate, even when the study is limited to negative peace, nor would all taken together provide a sufficient basis for comprehensive peace education.

There is no doubt that the general public does not understand the phenomenon of conflict or how to handle it constructively. Although arbitration, mediation, and negotiation are rapidly developing as professional fields, the average person has little capacity for and no training in conflict resolution at any level, from interpersonal through global. It is virtually inevitable, then, that as life and the world have become more complex and complicated, so too have they become more conflictual, and consequently more violent. The increased incidence of war in the twentieth century is but one aspect of an increase in all forms of violence, both overt and covert, including the ultimate violence — the threat of nuclear annihilation. Teachers are quite right in their insightful recognition that playground fights, school and community disorders, and domestic violence are interrelated. Nor do they need peace educators to provide the data and analysis documenting the interrelationships to see the necessity for education in conflict resolution. Violence is virtually never a means of resolving a conflict; at best it may terminate one phase of a conflict that will subsequently erupt again, as seen in the classic example, the two world wars. Violent conflict occurs because other modes of resolving conflict are not used. And the main reason for that is that most people, even at the highest levels of political leadership, are as ignorant of other modes of conflict resolution as they are of full and fundamental causes of conflict. This ignorance is itself a major cause of war. It is also a primary reason for advocating the rapid and widespread introduction of peace education into our schools and colleges.

Those who see the major causes of war as political and/or ideological generally focus on the relationship between the superpowers or on regional or civil struggles, such as those in Central America, Ethiopia, and Afghanistan. Their assumption about the causes of war, at least of current wars and the present threat of nuclear war, is that the roots of most armed conflict today are to be found mainly in the struggle between two political systems for power beyond their borders. Some view the primary political struggle as that between the poor and oppressed masses and the rich and powerful elites of the world. Some also see human rights violations and political repression as contributing factors. However, the programs that focus on these issues are far fewer than those that emphasize the American-Soviet or East-West conflict. In precollegiate education, more attention has been paid to industrial world–developing world (North-South) and civil conflicts, regional and local conflict in those programs that emphasize justice issues or take a more comprehensive approach, inclusive of concepts and concerns within the realm of positive peace.

By far the most widely considered set of issues in American public school peace education is the conflictual relationship between the United States and the Soviet Union, seen as the cause of the nuclear arms race and the threat of nuclear war. This emphasis on the superpower conflict as the major potential cause of war (particularly nuclear war) highlights two subjects: nuclear education and Soviet studies. These two subjects can be seen as natural descendants of the earlier preoccupation with the Soviet Union that gave rise to the educational fashion of instruction about Communism so common in American high schools in the fifties and sixties. Although the preoccupation did produce some very good curricular materials on the history and culture of the Soviet Union, this material was not nearly so popular as that which revealed the perverse fascination with the challenge of Communism to Western political and economic values. By and large, the graduates of those courses inspired by the cold war were no better informed about Soviet life and policy than the rest of the American public, which is so woefully ignorant of the past and present experiences of the Soviets.

This ignorance has become a profound concern of peace education. Current Soviet studies courses in universities and secondary schools reflect the assumption that war between the United States and the Soviet Union is most likely to result from blunders of miscommunication, miscalculation, and ignorance, shattering the delicate "balance of terror" maintained by nuclear deterrents. If the two powers were to know and understand each other better, they would be more likely to reach the accommodation necessary to maintain peace and avoid nuclear war. These assumptions, to some degree, arise from a notion of peace as international understanding and account for current programs in elementary schools that provide instruction about the lives of Russian children, Russian folktales and songs, and exchange of letters and art with Soviet children, as well as the study of Soviet life and culture in the higher grades.

For many of those who view the threat of nuclear war between the superpowers as the most significant area of concern, it is assumed that the probable cause of such a war would be the nuclear arms race. This assumption gave rise to the widely practiced current form of peace education that is called, by its practitioners, *nuclear education*. This form of education for negative peace has produced a voluminous popular literature on nuclear war as well as a number of major films and television programs, including dramas, documentaries, and panel discussions by experts. It has been taken up by many national and international professional associations, following the example of the physicians whose nuclear education efforts were recognized by the award of the 1984 UNESCO Peace Education Prize and the 1985 Nobel Peace Prize to the International Physicians for the Prevention of Nuclear War. The belief at the core of these efforts is that arms races themselves cause war. Major arms build-ups have preceded wars that might well have been avoided had not the belligerents been so well prepared to fight. Every weapon ever invented, it appears, has ultimately been used. And contrary to the theory of deterrence, the continued refinement and production of nuclear weapons is more likely to lead to war than to prevent it (Beer, 1983).

Those same assumptions also underlie the similar but broader field of *disarmament education* (UNESCO, 1980). That negative peace approach extends these assumptions to all arms, not just nuclear arms. Disarmament education takes a comprehensive view of the arms race and covers conventional weapons as well as all weapons of mass destruction, including new weapons now under design and development, that are far more exotic than those of the "strategic defense initiative" (SDI) but have received less public attention. This approach, more than any of the other negative peace approaches, comes closest to confronting the issue of war as an institution. It is a fairly global approach, bringing into consideration the notion of general and complete disarmament (GCD), the achievement of which would require all nations to renounce war. Disarmament education falls more into what I would categorize as a reconstructionist approach to peace education, because of the institutional requirements of GCD.

Nuclear education, in its exploration of reformist policy options, has tended to emphasize the nuclear freeze, the comprehensive test ban, and similar single-step arms control proposals as the major alternatives to the present escalating arms race, devoting only limited attention to other options in arms limitation and disarmament, and virtually none to general and complete disarmament. Disarmament education, however, looks at all options and explores more radical possibilities for change, such as alternative defense and security systems, changes that usually imply some restructuring of the international system and limits to national sovereignty. It inquires into a broad range of the ramifications of arms races and arms trade, including economic and social consequences and sociopolitical aspects of the problems. Disarmament education, still infrequently found in the schools, is presented mainly in the universities and in adult nonformal education, primarily in church-related programs and those of a few organizations such as the Jobs with Peace Campaign.

A major change in this situation may result from the work of the UN's World Disarmament Campaign, an education and information program working to facilitate disarmament education in all educational settings and in all parts of the world. The campaign was launched by the United Nations General Assembly during the opening days of the UN's Second Special Session on Disarmament in 1982. Its purpose is to inform, educate, and mobilize public opinion in favor of disarmament. To do so it offers materials and information to educational institutions, associations, and citizen organizations. It is a valuable resource to educators and activists. (For information, write to World Disarmament Campaign, c/o United Nations, New York, NY 10017.)

Current Purposes and Goals of Education for Negative Peace

The general purposes of current educational practices regarding negative peace are very similar to those espoused by the World Disarmament Campaign. The overall intent is, in fact, to develop a well-informed citizenry mobilized not only to favor but to take action toward the achievement of peace and disarmament. Although a fundamental goal is to inform, that is but the most basic of a broader range of purposes. Among them, the most evident appear to be to explain, to persuade, and to elicit response — purposes not usually listed among the learning objectives for peace education.

The most obvious and widely evident purpose has been to inform. Indeed it is this, the most simple and basic purpose of the field, that has gained the most public notice and the most severe criticism. The dissemination of fundamental information, previously unknown or ignored, regarding the nature, potential effects, and the current consequences of the development and stockpiling of nuclear weapons was the first and most widespread activity in the development of nuclear education. Although the field also presents facts concerning the nuclear arms race itself, the roles of both superpowers in the race, stages in weapons development, policy options for escalation or control, and study of the existing and potential conflicts that affect the nuclear predicament, it was the information on the probable effects of the use of nuclear weapons that gained the most attention and provoked the most severe criticism.

The charges leveled against nuclear education ranged from indoctrination to inflicting emotional damage on children. Indeed, it is possible that some instruction was presented as a one-sided argument for a nuclear freeze, and it is evident that many young children who had not previously demonstrated awareness of the problems were deeply disturbed by their newly acquired images of nuclear war. However, most peace education, whatever the particular approach, starts from the readiness of the learner to deal with the material. In fact, a number of nuclear education programs were first undertaken in response to the needs and desires expressed by students reacting to information garnered from sources outside the school. Since the objective most common to all approaches is the development of critical thinking, it appears that the criticism was really inspired by two circumstances not mentioned by the critics: the vigor and rapidity of the growth of the programs, and, most especially, their success. The basic objective of providing the information was obviously being achieved: Learners were moving beyond the passive acceptance of the nuclear threat, as evidenced by student actions for peace and disarmament. Students became active in the larger peace movement and also undertook student-initiated and -directed efforts to reach other students and the general public.

Other evidence of such a movement is the readiness of learners to receive instruction intended to explain not only the dynamics and circumstances of the arms race but its causes, the characteristics of the international system in which it operates, and the nature of the relationships among nations in conflict. Particularly at the upper secondary level, the complexities of the political and ethical questions are sometimes addressed. Even with younger children the value questions raised by problems in relationships and the creative possibilities of multiple responses to conflict situations can be dealt with so that learners have both an understanding of the complexities and a behavioral repertoire that frees them from the restrictions of the simplistic either–or approach often taken by national leaders. The objective is to help learners to develop the ability to engage in a reasoned critique of the situations and the policy responses to them. It was largely this form of reasoned critique that led to student action.

Peace educators generally agree that critical analysis is most useful when it is applied to actual problem solving. A major need in the field is to persuade students and the public alike that the problems that are obstacles to peace can be resolved. This is not to argue that there is an ultimate solution or a technological fix for every problem but only to illustrate that although there is no simple answer, such problems can be approached in ways that avoid their most negative consequences. Nuclear weapons are such a problem (Jacobson et al., 1983). The assumption that most global problems, even those of the proportions of the nuclear threat, are humanly derived and can be overcome by human intervention is common to all approaches. Nuclear education seeks to persuade that the danger is too great to be left at the present impasse. Disarmament education seeks to persuade that fundamental policy changes could change the basic situation. International understanding seeks to persuade that all peoples are human, have the same desire to survive, and have a common stake in avoiding war. Conflict studies seeks to persuade that even though conflict is probably inevitable, violence is not, and that there are nondestructive ways in which nations can compete and resolve disputes. All seek the same learning objective, a positive problem-solving approach (Jacobson, 1982). They seek to persuade learners not of the efficacy of particular solutions but of the range of possibilities to be found in the human capacity for problem solving. In their pursuit of the development of this capacity, all forms of education for negative peace are educating for global responsibility.

It is this approach that makes it possible for peace educators to describe their goal as eliciting (not imposing or inculcating) positive responses, recognizing that education is not so much a process of imparting knowledge as it is "drawing out" the capacity to learn. Peace education, whether limited to negative peace or encompassing positive peace, needs to elicit awareness and understanding of the problems of war and violence. These objectives, sometimes described as consciousness-raising, however, are in most cases seen as preliminary to other objectives—the use of imagination and planning, the development of values, and commitment to action. In eliciting awareness, the intent is to strengthen the capacity to care, to develop a sincere concern for those who suffer because of the problems and a commitment to resolving them through action. Awareness infused by caring becomes concern that can lead to such commitment when one action is followed by other actions, and when action for peace becomes a sustained behavioral pattern, part of the learner's way of life (Laor, 1980). The objective is to elicit an ongoing and active response to the problems of peace and a commitment to their resolution. As I will outline later, this cycle of care, concern, and commitment is the core of the peace learning process.

Political Issues: The Problem of Indoctrination

The values and action dimensions of peace education have been a significant source of controversy—controversy that needs to be confronted head-on by peace educators. When the purposes include persuasion, then the questions of indoctrination and bias must be addressed. Accusations of bias have been leveled at peace education and peace studies from many sides, by academics as well as by professional unions and school administrations. Unfortunately most of these accusations, and most of the other criticisms mentioned earlier, stem from the prevailing pattern of dualistic, either-or thinking that permeates our culture and our politics, reflecting the fallacious notion that to be objective means to be value-free. Fortunately there are few educators who still cling to the notion that any education can be value-free. Most, as Paolo Freire (1973) asserts, agree that there is no neutral education. Education is a social enterprise conducted for the realization of social values. The question is what values are to be realized through education, and how. What do peace educators view as the appropriate relation between social values and pedagogical values?

Clearly peace education places a high social value on the reduction of organized violence and the avoidance of war. These ends may be stated as the primary value goals of education for negative peace. We seek to educate for their achievement, as other generations and fields of education have sought to contribute to other social goals, such as improved public health, national cohesion, and a productive economy. Such accepted educational goals were admittedly far from neutral, and certainly not value-free. The values concerned were socially sanctioned, and the schools were not accused of indoctrination when they tried to impart them. Few thoughtful educators would doubt, however, that deliberate inculcation and indoctrination were used in some instances. Of most concern is the effectiveness of such methods. Can indoctrination truly serve the purposes of peace education? For those peace educators for whom the development of critical consciousness is a major learning objective, and most especially those who see it as a fundamental educational purpose, the answer is an unequivocal no. But this raises the even more controversial issue of what values our society holds in regard to war and violence. It is the raising of this question in a critical context that is, I would argue, the basic reason for the charges against peace education.

Clearly, neither education nor educators are neutral, nor should they aspire to be. On the other hand, we do want to avoid specific political biases and lack of objectivity. If peace education programs do in fact advocate specific formulas for achieving peace, rather than inquiring into as many proposals as possible, in order to help students develop critical consciousness and determine for themselves which they will decide to advocate, then such programs are not only biased—they are not good peace education. The ultimate goal of peace education is the achievement of peace, not the adoption of some specific route to peace. If well-informed critical judgments are to be made, then all possibilities must be objectively examined, using generally accepted standards of both scholarship and public policy formation. The objectives of reasoned critique and ongoing active political response cannot be separated, particularly since peace education is largely political education, education for citizenship. And this is the heart of the problem. Are the schools really intended to prepare for active participation in a democratic political process?

The potential for political action inherent in this form of education provides grist for the critics' mill. Yet the criticism is welcome, for it opens both the issues and the questions of how to educate about them to much-needed public discussion. The danger lies in the efforts of some critics to remove the issues from the arena of public discourse by using pressure to close off this vital inquiry in our schools. Ongoing engagement of the critics is a significant need in our field.

The needs in the broad field of peace education must also be taken into account as we struggle for clarity of purpose and content. This review of the approaches used in negative peace education is intended to stimulate a wider discussion of definitions, approaches, and problems faced by all peace education. In the view of many individuals and organizations associated with the peace, social change, and futurist movements, humanity is experiencing today some of the most far-reaching changes since the industrial revolution — perhaps since the emergence of settled economic production itself. For the first time in human history, human beings have the capacity to destroy the entire planet. There is no question that this is a time of significant choices for the human species. Peace is the major, global survival issue of our times. The scope and depth of the field of peace education must be made equal to the task of meeting this challenge. The challenge calls for peace education to be comprehensive, transformational, and pragmatic; to continue to emphasize the practical, hardheaded concerns comprehended within the domain of negative peace but to include as well the particularly human concerns that comprise positive peace.

Comprehensive, authentic peace — the convergence of positive and negative peace — is, indeed, a utopian concept. But we must remember that the purposes of utopias are to clearly expose the follies and crimes of the existing order while providing us with images of alternatives, so as to inspire action for change. At base, peace education must be education for action. We need to educate for change — for practical, achievable change. For the realm of negative peace, that change means, at a minimum, severely reducing the likelihood of war, and optimally it means the abolition of war.

Thus, peace education must be pragmatic, but its pragmatism must go beyond those present practical approaches that offer instruction only about policy options derived within the present system, the mode of reformist peace education. It must now emphasize, in a reconstructionist manner, learning to change systems and institutions, particularly the systems through which the Earth's resources are distributed, the world economic system, and that system in which nations compete over those resources, the war system. Peace education must confront the need to abolish the institution of war: Otherwise it will not be an agent of transformation. One practical step we can take to develop a field capable of meeting its challenge is to redefine negative peace so as to mean the total abolition of war as a human institution, and positive peace as a social order in which the resort to armed conflict is no longer to be expected, and certainly not to be accepted. Such a step would also move us toward a transformational approach to peace education and a more comprehensive definition of the field.

CHAPTER 3

Education for Positive Peace

Positive peace has become the concept connoting a world in which the need for violence has been significantly reduced; if not eliminated. The major areas of concern in the domain of positive peace are the problems of economic deprivation and development; environment and resources; and universal human rights and social justice. Peace education seems to have subsumed all of these areas into the general concept of global justice. Although the term *global justice*, as it is used by classroom teachers, is not as precise as the term *positive peace*, it is appropriate, since "justice," in the sense of the full enjoyment of the entire range of human rights by all people, is what constitutes positive peace.

Global Justice: The Central Concept of Positive Peace

Global justice is a comprehensive concept in which changes in global social and economic systems are seen as the necessary preconditions for authentic world peace. Indeed, it appears that more peace educators may be focusing on questions related to the global environment and to the inequities in the world economic system than are teaching about war. The reasons for this are to be found in some of the leading foreign-policy questions facing the American public and in the pedagogical possibilities offered by the problems of world poverty.

Although the urgency of the issues of the nuclear arms race and American–Soviet relations has resulted in those particular questions taking center stage in American peace education programs, the questions raised by Central American liberation struggles, the African famine, and the antiapartheid movement have also been increasingly reflected in school curricula. Problems of injustice are accorded great significance by peace educators.

The study of forms of injustice, particularly poverty, appears to be approached in two distinct manners: problem-centered and structural. The problem-centered is the more widely used approach in North America. The structural approach, more common in Europe and Latin America, appears most often in curricula developed by educators whose work is grounded in religious faith, particularly Roman Catholic educators such as those in the Leaven movement or the Peace and Justice Education Council (Reardon, 1988). It also appears in the work of those whose approaches have been developed in international settings. (See annotated listings of Special Peace Education issues of the *Bulletin of Peace Proposals* in the Appendix.)

The study of global economic inequities is another area in which the concept of structural violence and the analysis of social values are especially relevant. The analysis of injustice in the global economic system, like the analysis of the frequent recourse to violence in conflicts, demands that values be addressed. Growing world hunger, existing simultaneously with agricultural surplus; inadequate income, among workers in areas that produce widely consumed raw materials; the need of some nations to import expensive manufactured items made of materials that they themselves have produced; the simultaneous increase, in certain countries, of the gross national product and of the number of people falling into poverty: Such contrasts raise issues to be analyzed so as to provide an understanding of the structures controlling the global economy. The circumstances that account for such paradoxical problems of human want in a world of plenty demand, as well, an analysis of the values underlying the policies that permit these problems to continue. Indeed, these problems allow for structural and policy analysis at all levels, local to global, and they call, too, for values analysis at all levels, including the personal and individual. While developing capacities to make judgments on public policy, students, starting at the secondary level, can also examine their own social and political values. Since most of these issues can be traced through the global network to the points at which they affect and are affected by individuals, students can come to understand their own place in these global structures and can explore their own behaviors and values, deciding whether they wish to act for change. Choosing among the range of options for action is in itself an exercise in values analysis and decision making. Identifying the options is also an empowering process. Thus two significant learning goals of peace education are met: the acquisition of decision-making skills, and the development of a sense of empowerment. Both goals featured prominently in the curricula submitted to the curriculum survey (Reardon, 1988).

Curricular Antecedents of Education for Positive Peace

Exploring the notions of positive peace that inform current practices in peace education provides an opportunity to observe the positive roots of this curricular area. Just as the recent educational preoccupations with the nuclear arms race and the Soviet Union have their antecedents in earlier concerns with Soviet expansionism and the spread of Communism, so the concern with global justice has precedents from earlier, more positive concepts of *education for international understanding, international education*, and *global education.*

Education for international understanding was probably the earliest form of education for positive peace. The notion of negative peace sometimes leads to emphasis on differences, and to a concern for understanding adversaries so as to "handle" them in competitive or conflictual situations. The notion of positive peace, on the other hand, calls for emphasis on commonalities and on understanding others so as to cooperate with them. Although the assumption that increased understanding will inevitably lead to more harmonious and cooperative relationships is open to question, the premise of educating for cooperation rather than competition was significant in the development of education for positive peace. Some of the early efforts in education for international understanding may have lacked real substance. A few probably even contributed to reinforcing old stereotypes or creating new ones, such as the problematic and negative view of the developing world. However, the basic purpose was to learn to understand others, in order to bring about a new and more positive system of international relations, with increased cooperation and reduced international conflict. The fundamental assumption was that although nations and groups differed widely, all people were equally human, and that if we got to know others, we would recognize this fact and act accordingly. What was missing was the substance of "acting accordingly," as well as study of the systems and process that would make such action possible. Education for international understanding and its companion, *international education*, instruction about other nations that was designed to provide knowledge suitable for the newly acquired international responsibilities of the United States, was the most popular approach in the 1940s and 1950s. During this period there were also increased efforts to provide "international" experience through exchange visits and to prepare students for "international" careers. Even today the term *international* is commonly used in relation to events and efforts that are in fact *transnational*, or global. Our familiar use of the term *international* for activities and concerns that go beyond national boundaries reflects the fact that for many of us, our only way of identifying with the larger world is through national identities; thus *international* has a functional connotation of interactions among persons from various cultures and nations that *transnational* and *global* do not. (The pity is that many of our national leaders have this perspective.)

Two other approaches to international education, especially popular during the fifties, which shared similar assumptions and purposes, were *area studies*—in-depth study of particular world regions—and *multicultural education*, which emphasized the study of peoples of the so-called non–Western world and of minority cultures in the United States. Multicultural studies still has some currency in peace education, but area studies, because it lacked a global perspective and had little focus on global problems, was never really incorporated into peace education.

Neither have had as much impact as *global education*. The assumptions about the importance of the commonalities among all peoples characteristic of education for international understanding were carried into global education, which emerged in the sixties. Conceptually it differed from international understanding in several ways. Whereas the earlier approach illuminated the multiplicity of human cultures, nations, and political systems (usually viewed in a comparative perspective), global education made evident the interdependence of all human groups and the realities of one planetary system, summed up in the notions of interdependence and Spaceship Earth. It, too, emphasized the possibilities for cooperation and the necessity of recognizing that contemporary public problems were, by and large, global problems, requiring global solutions, which in turn required global cooperation. Some global education, however, in its earlier phases attempted to emulate one tradition of its parent discipline, social science. It sometimes claimed to be neutral and value-free, at least in its study of global problems, and ignored or rejected considerations of restructuring the international system. Some who identified themselves as peace educators saw this as a major distinction between the two fields, much as peace and world order studies practitioners at the university level distinguished their work from the more traditional field of international relations (Weston et al., 1978). Peace studies and peace education have always been self-described as normative fields, acknowledging an explicit value base (Thorpe & Reardon, 1971). Positive peace is an especially value-laden area, and current global education certainly is value-laden and emphasizes problems that involve many value questions (Kniep, 1986). Indeed, as they appear in the teacher-developed curricula submitted to the World Policy Institute survey (Reardon, 1988), notions of positive peace, in units identified as global education, emphasize value concepts.

Notions of Positive Peace

That positive peace emphasizes affective and values education can also be seen in the core concepts that many of the survey respondents identified as the basis of their curricula. These concepts tended to cluster around three value sets: communal and civic values, life-affirming values, and the value of the human person and positive human relationships. A conceptual shorthand for the three value clusters are the terms *citizenship, stewardship*, and *relationships*. (These concepts will be discussed further in Chapter 5, in relation to the goals and purposes of peace education.) These core values infuse most of the concepts and notions of positive peace revealed in the peace education curriculum survey.

In survey responses, the frequent mention of community building as a peacemaking process, the emphasis on the human commonalities that transcend cultural, national, and ideological differences, and the assertion of the imperative of a common planetary future for all peoples seemed to manifest the notion of peace as community. There are frequent references in the curricula and in the theoretical literature, to global community as the conceptual core of a peaceful world society (Matriano & Reardon, 1976). "Community" is conceived as the recognition of common destiny and common welfare. The concept of community is reinforced by the emphasis on caring, sharing, cooperation, and solidarity as values and attitudes pursued among the affective objectives of peace education. These values are also seen as essential to the achievement of global justice and are fundamental to development education. The achievement of these values is dependent upon our willingness and our capacities to contribute to the building of the global community, to behave with a sense of global civic responsibility, and to see ourselves as global citizens.

Peace as a network of humane relationships based on equity, mutuality, and the inherent worth of all persons might be interpreted as the manifestation of global justice. This concept of peace seems to be the one that is most characteristic of multicultural approaches to peace education that seek to develop appreciation of cultural differences and recognition of human dignity as the essential basis for human relations — interpersonal, social, and structural. It is, as well, the value base that informs human rights education.

Peace as affirmation of life is probably the most powerful and dynamic notion of positive peace. Since the goal of a global community implies the need for structural change, and since the achievement of truly equitable, mutual human relationships calls for conscious changes in values and attitudes, then affirming life, in our current circumstances, requires active struggle. It calls for struggle against the endemic poverty that shortens life and lowers the quality of life for the majority of the earth's peoples; against the chronic hunger and famine that sap the strength and extinguish the lives of millions; against a conventional arms race that saps resources and promotes lethal conflict within and among nations throughout the world; and against the proliferation of nuclear weapons that threatens the life of Earth itself. The preservation of the Earth is the foremost goal of those who hold this concept of peace, and it usually involves redefining the relationships between human beings and the planet. These struggles are all part of a worldwide movement to create what a Chilean peace educator has called the "culture of life" (Vio Grossi, 1985). All of the various efforts to achieve human dignity for all people and to realize a viable global society on an ecologically healthy planet are part of this movement. The "green" movements around the world, which began with environmental concerns and expanded into related structural issues, are the outstanding example of such efforts. Environmental education is also a significant factor in this trend, especially as it relates to developing a concern for the health of the planet. All have also had some influence on education for positive peace.

Positive Peace: Approaches and Concerns

Enhancing the quality of life is a fundamental goal of three curricular approaches that I would classify as part of education for positive peace: *environmental education, development education*, and *human rights education*. The first two appear to be more widely practiced than the third. Not all who teach in these areas consider themselves to be peace educators, nor indeed are they. Whether a curriculum in any of these areas can be classified as peace education depends on its value content and its treatment of the core problems addressed by peace education: violence.

Among curricula in each of these three general approaches can be found curricular examples that reflect the notion of violence as "intentional and avoidable damage to life, or injury to life-sustaining or life-enhancing elements of the environment or social structures." In environmental education, for example, the term *ecocide*, meaning the total destruction of the ecosphere, connotes that the environment, particularly when conceived as a living ecological system, can be the victim or object of violence. In development studies, the term *structural violence* is used to describe the limits to human life and well-being imposed by inequitable economic structures revealing a growing acceptance of the assertion that some forms of indirect violence are inflicted by social and economic institutions. In human rights education, the term *violation* is used to describe the denial or abuse of rights, particularly civil and political rights, reflecting the notion that life-diminishing damage can be perpetrated by forces other than weaponry and armed struggle.

Nearly all forms of environmental education, development education, and human rights education are based on explicit values. *Environmental education* is based on the value of preserving the ecosystem, *development education* on the value of increasing material well-being, and *human rights education* on the value of recognizing the dignity and worth of all human beings. Those forms of the three that fall within the sphere of education for positive peace confront value conflicts and call for values analysis at both the personal and structural levels. On the personal level, the value questions are analyzed from the perspective of individual behaviors and life-style choices, and on the structural level from that of alternatives for public policy and public institutions. Among the learning goals of such education are stimulating awareness of the values implicit in individual behaviors and public policy proposals; building comprehension of the value conflicts involved in the formulation and execution of public policy and in personal adherence to public policy; and developing sensitivity to the inconsistencies in our values that affect our personal lives and subvert the articulated human and social values of our political system. Deeply embedded in all of these approaches is the assumption that the achievement of positive peace requires consistency of values and that certain core values must be pursued at all levels of social organization and in all areas of human experience.

The explicitness of the values expressed in education for positive peace make it even more controversial than education for negative peace. Americans generally are not familiar with social-structural analysis, and the concept of structural violence is alien to most. To many, such social analysis sounds like Marxism, creating much suspicion and concern. Many people also fail to distinguish between the "sinner" and the "sin." Political parties, ideological factions, social classes or movements, and particular persons are seen as the causes of the problem; consequently, solutions are projected in terms of dealing with such elements, rather than with the structures that condition or make possible their behaviors. These concerns are especially strong where economic structures are brought under analysis. The conflicts that often develop between the values of economic equity and "free enterprise," between the ethos of individualism and independence and that of the "common welfare" and "interdependence," become even more intense when the analysis concerns the entire world. If education for negative peace has been viewed as unpatriotic because of the issues it raises, education for positive peace may be seen as downright dangerous, a challenge to our way of life.

This raises the issue of whether education should call prevailing social values into question or assess the relationship between the society's articulated values and the social reality. Such critical questioning, although it often leads to accusations of bias, is the very process that our leading educational philosophers have advocated as the primary purpose of public education (Paulo Freire and John Dewey, for example, as noted by one peace educator [O'Hare, 1983]). That the continued development of the capacity for critical thinking should be part of lifelong learning is indicated by the centrality of that capacity to adult education. A significant component of critical thinking is the ability to detect bias in the presentation of information (Brookfield, 1986).

Education regarding public issues has always been controversial and open to accusations of indoctrination. Responsible education, it is asserted, requires the study of "both sides" of any issue. The assumption is that unbiased education means giving equal consideration to opposing biases. However, it becomes more and more apparent that the major public issues we face are complex and many-sided, and that to reduce consideration of views to the two most in opposition to each other is hardly adequate. Most good peace education is sensitive to this reality and offers multiple views of problems, and multiple alternative solutions. Education for the analysis of controversial issues has been acknowledged as a central responsibility of our schools for over two decades (Oliver & Shaver, 1974), and it has been a significant component of the kind of citizenship education espoused by peace educators.

Such citizenship education includes instruction in ways of uncovering bias. Just as there is a distinction between objectivity and neutrality, so there is also one between a value stance and a bias. Although teachers need not pretend to neutrality, they can and should attempt to avoid bias and to achieve objectivity. Objectivity means looking at all the evidence, so as to know as much of the truth of a situation as is possible. This does not mean that evidence is weighed without regard to values. Certainly values are crucial to any assessment of evidence, but the values must be acknowledged and factored into the assessment. Bias, however, precludes objectivity, excludes data that does not support its positions, and distorts evidence rather than fully examine it. Bias seldom admits its value base and prevents full consideration and fair assessment of all relevant data and opinion on the issue under study. To be *neutral* is to be without authentic concern for an issue or for the values that it brings into play. To be *biased* is to deny the multiplicity of concerns that affect an issue and to deny the relevance of values. Objectivity is often bias disguised by ignoring value issues. Effective peace educators cannot be biased; nor can they be neutral. It is far more objective for peace educators to reveal their own values and lay them open to examination than to make inadequate attempts to veil them with the stance of neutrality. The issues raised in peace education, particularly the issues raised by problems of positive peace, require that the values of teachers and students, as well as those of policy advocates, be fully explored and assessed. Toward that end, I find the following sequence of value-clarification questions, proposed by Walbek and Weiss, most useful:

1) Which values are most important? How are they defined and justified?
2) Is there an explicit or implicit hierarchy of values? How are actual or potential value conflicts resolved?
3) How conscious and reflective is one about the consequences of personal value positions upon the subsequent perception of reality, definitions of the purposes for study and research, and choice of problem-solving methodology?
4) Is there a sensitivity and explicit awareness about the influences of culture and class background in defining personal values? To what extent can one attempt to correct for or include other class and cultural frames of reference? (Walbek & Weiss, 1974)

The significance of an acknowledged value stance is especially pertinent to the most clear and concrete, yet the most neglected area of education for positive peace, human rights. To stand openly and firmly in favor of human rights, particularly civil and political rights, is very much within the accepted American political and social tradition. U.S. foreign policy on human rights, however, has become an issue of public debate. However, even though the topic is covered by the popular media, it has yet to achieve a significant place in American peace education. (Some notable exceptions are the curricular material produced by the Center for Peace and Conflict Studies, of Wayne State University in Detroit, and some newly devised curricular materials for global education; for a description of the Center's materials, see "Recommended Curriculum Materials" in Reardon, 1988.) Neither the materials submitted to the survey nor most of those commercially available offered much opportunity to introduce the subject into school classrooms.

There are several reasons why this lack of attention to human rights issues is a serious omission. First, the concept of universal human rights and the original international instruments that defined them stem from our own political traditions. Indeed, the Universal Declaration of Human Rights, adopted by consensus by the United Nations General Assembly in 1948, was largely the result of the efforts of an American rights advocate and diplomat, Eleanor Roosevelt. Second, the concepts of rights, as well as the specific rights enumerated in international documents, constitute an excellent yardstick by which to measure the quality-of-life factors central to the study of positive peace. Third, the Universal Declaration of

Human Rights is an ideal vehicle through which to introduce concepts of globalism and world problems into standard history and social studies courses. Fourth, denial of human rights is the major source of conflict and obstacle to peace in many areas of the developing world. Finally, the covenants, conventions, declarations, and laws related to human rights are an excellent source of specific facts and concepts to use in conceptualizing and imaging a peaceful and just society. They provide a means though which the abstract values and utopian visions of a preferred future can be turned into concrete proposals and precise images. They are at once an effective diagnostic device for assessing violence and injustice and a promising prescriptive mechanism for describing the conditions of positive peace. Few would argue against the notion that a world in which human rights were fully, consistently, and universally respected would be a world at peace.

Human rights is a rich curricular area for peace education and the most promising conceptual area for linking positive and negative peace (Marks, 1983).

Topical Themes and Curricular Titles

Peace education curricula are not always described in terms of the concepts and approaches outlined here. A brief review of the more popular themes and titles may therefore help to provide a more familiar context. It would seem that a truly comprehensive approach must include some elements from each, since each centers on a concern essential to peacemaking.

The most widely used descriptor, and undoubtedly the most widely practiced approach to education for peace, is still *global education*. Here the concern is mainly with the nature of global interdependence and with seeing the world as a single system and understanding the global dimensions of public issues. Global education is probably the most varied and least focused of all current approaches.

Both the survey and my own observation lead me to believe that the second most popular themes are *nuclear education* and *conflict resolution*. Most public school programs in these areas derive from guidelines laid down by state or local boards of education and/or by professional associations (such as the National Education Association or the National Council for the Social Studies) and are identified as "conflict resolution," "nuclear" (or "nuclear age") education, and "global" education.

Conflict resolution, as I noted in Chapter 2, emphasizes techniques for the constructive management of conflict and is centered on a concern with conflict as a characteristic of all human relations, from the personal to the global. Nuclear education is primarily centered on a concern about nuclear weapons and the threat of nuclear war. It explores the facts about these two issues, as well as nuclear fears and related concerns about nuclear power and the cold war. This field, developed by Educators for Social Responsibility, has been deepened and broadened to include what is now called "nuclear age education," which deals with a wider range of global problems and conflicts.

Peace education, however, which began as the study of the causes of war and the possibilities for preventing it, has broadened its scope so much that its central concern, as we have seen, is now the whole phenomenon of violence in most of its manifestations, from the personal to the global. Given the nature of global problems (even those basic to environmental education, development education, and the much less prominent field of human rights education), peace education has, it seems to me, a greater potential as a starting point for a truly comprehensive approach to education for global transformation than the others, except for nuclear age education.

The concern for a more comprehensive approach led, in the mid-seventies, to the articulation of *global community education* (Matriano & Reardon, 1976). Global community education was designed to build upon the broad and well-integrated value base provided by world order studies and to expand its cultural and personal dimensions. Its developers attempted to formulate a more fully multidisciplinary, humanistic, comprehensive approach and to integrate materials, methods, and insights from multicultural education with the methods of inquiry of world order studies. Although very few educators have used this approach, there are indications that a trend emerging from similar views of global and nuclear education is now under way.

Nuclear age education has come to be quite similar to global community education. Both have as a major goal the building of a viable global order. Thus the original differences among curricular areas are beginning to blur. The 1986 national conference of Educators for Social Responsibility, the major proponent of nuclear age education, treated themes far more varied than nuclear issues, offering sessions on apartheid, women's issues, ecology, and various other global problems. The goals are not limited to education for understanding global issues but also include the achievement of globally viable resolution of world problems. There are indications that certain elements of a reconstructive approach are being incorporated into nuclear age education. Although not as explicit in its values (i.e., not emphasizing particular norms such as the five world order values) nor so focused on structural analysis as are world order studies and other reconstructive approaches, and still reluctant to be designated as peace education, there are undeniably normative and change-oriented elements in these broader approaches. Perhaps the time has come to consider integrating all of these approaches into a comprehensive approach to peace education for global responsibility in a nuclear age.

CHAPTER 4

Peace Knowledge: Content and Context

Sources of Peace Knowledge

The notion that we know little or nothing about peace has been a major stumbling block to the development of broad public support for peace education. Responsible educators could hardly advocate the initiation of programs for which there is no knowledge base. This popular notion of ignorance in the realm of peace is far from true. We have a broad knowledge base, one more than adequate to meet current needs for comprehensive, integrated peace education for global responsibility in a nuclear age.

I have suggested that the primary source of knowledge about the causes of war and the conditions of peace is the field of peace research. Yet when planning a curriculum for the schools, the broadest possible knowledge base should be sought. Although peace research should rightly be considered as the basis for the academic and scholarly study of peace, and should, I believe, play a more important role in curriculum development, there are two other equally important sources of peace knowledge.

One of these sources is the United Nations, which, in pursuit of its goal of avoiding the "scourge of war," has gained much practical experience and produced many outstanding scientific studies. Yet this rich source of information and experience receives very little attention in the curricula of our schools and universities. It is important for peace education to integrate this knowledge into a curriculum that will put it to practical use in the struggle for peace, for it has been produced in the actual day-to-day struggle for peace.

The successes of the work of the UN are generally overlooked by the popular media and are seldom considered in reviews of possibilities for a peaceful world. Yet the UN is our major global political body, the one institution intentionally dedicated to the welfare of the whole of humanity, a purpose to which thousands within the institution have committed long and often arduous years of service. Although the American media have focused on the diplomatic functions of the organization, the social glitter and political intrigue associated with diplomacy, and some short-comings in administration and finance, and have emphasized the UN's failure to prevent all armed conflict to guarantee negative peace, the UN has made remarkable, unheralded strides in the struggle for positive peace. It is the agency that has defined for us in functional, practical terms what a global problem is. In its pursuit of knowledge about the problems and the possibilities for their resolution, it has in less than fifty years accumulated a store of data about the world greater than all we had prior to its establishment (Childers, 1985). It may well be the most signifi-cant storehouse of human knowledge since the library of the ancient world at Alexandria. And, for all the attention given it by the public and educators, one would think it too had been burned to extinction.

I believe the United Nations should have a much more prominent place in all global education and should be heavily emphasized in peace education, because it is the major institution through which the skills and arts of peacemaking are practiced. As the primary arena for the exercise of civic responsibility at the global level, the United Nations provides the norms and standards for the pursuit and protection of the fundamental rights of all peoples. No other forum exists in which all systems and cultures can explore differences peacefully; only through the UN can all nations strive to create a viable and just world polity (Reardon, 1987).

There is also a third, generally ignored source of peace knowledge: human experience itself. This is an experience not usually reflected in our history texts. However, it seems evident that we must possess a vast knowledge of problem solving and conflict resolution, for without it our species could not possibly have survived to this date and to these times in which we seem to have forgotten so much of what the experience of other generations should have taught us. This practical human knowledge could be reclaimed by peace education, particularly in its emphasis on the multicultural heritage of humankind.

It is reason, too, for peace education to insist that the history we teach reclaim the experience of women in their daily contributions to creating the conditions of peace and resolving the untold number of conflicts that never erupted into war (E. Boulding, 1976). It is also proper cause for peace education to include women's studies (Reardon, 1985) and women's socialization processes (Brock-Utne, 1985). Certainly peace educators and researchers should support Kenneth Boulding's proposal (1986) that we research the history of peace as an essential component of our curriculum-development process. Finally, we must recognize that the Western, industrial, masculine bias that has closed out the historical experience of most of the world's peoples has made of history, as it has thus far been recorded and taught, a discipline that impedes rather than contributes to peace knowledge.

A World Core Curriculum: A Truly Comprehensive Approach

I find these assumptions about peace knowledge derived from the United Nations and the human experience reflected in the World Core Curriculum (n.d.) outlined by Robert Muller, former UN under secretary general. Although his proposal seems so broad as to complicate the tasks of the definition and delimitation of peace education, it seems to me to be the only recommendation that is comprehensive enough, especially in its time and space perspectives, for the task. One of the crucial but unrecognized obstacles to the development of a truly global perspective is the comparatively narrow conceptual base from which most peace education has started. It is important that peace education for the end of the twentieth century be designed to take account of the broadest possible context of time, space, and human experience. In the following excerpts from Muller's curriculum as one example, note not only this breadth of context but also his emphasis on pattern and relationship and how he points out the opportunities, as well as the need, to educate for global citizenship and planetary stewardship.

I. Our Planetary Home and Place in the Universe

The first major segment of my curriculum would deal with our prodigious knowledge of planet Earth. Humanity has been able, of late, to produce a magnificent picture of our planet and of its place in the universe.

From the infinitely large to the infinitely small, everything fits today in a very simple and clear pattern. . . .

The framework allows us to present our planetary and universal knowledge to all people and particularly to children in a simple, beautiful way. They wish to be told about their correct place in the universe. The Greeks' and Pascal's genial view of the infinitely large and the infinitely small has been filled in by science and provides the framework for much of today's world cooperation and daily lives of peoples. We can now give children a breathtaking view of the beauty and teeming, endless richness of Creation as has never been possible before. It should make them glad to be alive and to be human. . . .

. . . This gives the teachers of this world a marvelous opportunity to teach children and people a sense of participation and responsibility in the building and management of the Earth, of being artisans of our further human ascent. A new world morality and world ethics will thus evolve all along the above scale, and teachers will be able to prepare responsible citizens, workers, scientists, geneticists, physicists, and scores of other professions, including a new one which is badly needed: good world managers and caretakers.

II. The Human Family

There is a second segment on which humanity has also made tremendous progress of late: not only have we taken cognizance of our planet and of our place in the universe, but we have also taken stock of ourselves! This is of momentous importance, for henceforth our story in the universe is basically that of ourselves and of our planet. For a proper unfolding of that story, we had to know its two main elements well: the planet and ourselves. This has been accomplished since World War II. The planetary and human inventories are now practically complete.

III. Our Place in Time

In the same way as humanity is taking cognizance of its correct place in the universe, we are now also forced to look at our correct place in time or eternity.

. . . Thus humanity is forced to expand its time dimension tremendously both into the past and into the future: we must preserve the natural elements inherited from the past and necessary for our life and survival (air, water, soils, energy, animals, fauna, flora, genetic materials). We also want to preserve our cultural heritage, the landmarks of our own evolution and history in order to see the unfolding and magnitude of our cosmic journey. At the same time, we must think and plan far ahead into the future in order to hand over to coming generations a well preserved and better managed planet in the universe. What does this mean for a world curriculum? It means that we must add a time dimension to the above layers, each of which has a past, a present, and a future. . . .

IV. The Miracle and Fulfillment of Individual Life

It is becoming increasingly clear that in this vast evolutionary quantum change the individual remains the alpha and the omega of all our efforts. Individual human life is the highest form of universal consciousness on our planet. Institutions, concepts, factories, systems, states, ideologies, theories have no consciousness. They are all servants, instruments, means for better lives and the increase of individual human consciousness.

We are faced today with the full-fledged centrality, dignity, miracle, sanctity or divinity of individual human life, irrespective of race, sex, status, age, nation, physical or mental capacity.

. . . An immense global task and responsibility thus [awaits] all teachers and educators of this planet: it is no less than to contribute to the survival and good management of our planetary home and species, to our further common ascent into a universal, interdependent, peaceful civilization, while ensuring the knowledge, skills and fulfillment of all human beings prepared for life by the Earth's schools. . . .

Clearly the scope and vision of the World Core Curriculum should be kept in mind as we seek to construct an appropriate conceptual framework for peace education.

A Conceptual Framework: The University for Peace Curriculum Outline

We seek a conceptual framework that offers both breadth and coherence: wide enough to comprehend all of the relevant problems but systematic enough to illuminate the interrelationships among them and to provide conceptual clarity for the inquiry into their resolution. One outline for education for peace that currently offers such parameters is that of the University for Peace. This international institution of higher learning, based in Costa Rica, was established by the United Nations in 1980 to implement the purpose expressed in the university's motto, "If you want peace, prepare for peace." During the first planning phase, the university's council (on which I served from 1983 to 1986) and staff conducted a study of the content and practice of peace education programs around the world. From a long and varied list of topics and approaches, a general conceptual framework was distilled to serve as a possible framework for curriculum development. This conceptual framework, adopted by the council of the university in January 1985, serves as a useful general statement of the content of the field. The selection of global problems that it presents is derived from a problem analysis based on the world order values derived by the World Order Models Project, and the two other categories reflect some of the same concerns that led to the formulation of the global community approach.

The comments that follow reflect what I believe to be the promising beginning for a process of conceptual definition. Although designed for a university, it can also serve as a useful basis for curriculum development at all educational levels. These comments are adapted from a paper that I presented to the International Association of University Presidents in 1984 (Reardon, 1984).

The substantive areas of study on which the curriculum is currently being planned fall in three general conceptual areas, designated as: *quality of life*, dealing with social, economic, and cultural topics and issues;

planetary civic order, dealing with the political, administrative, and organizational aspects of the international order; and the *global problematique*, dealing with the major impediments to world peace. The core values and guiding purposes of the University for Peace are reflected in these three conceptual areas. The university's fundamental purpose is to offer an education that can contribute to the achievement of a just and peaceful planetary social order and to an improved quality of life for all members of the human family. These two objectives are the conceptual basis for the topics addressed in the curriculum.

Under the rubric "quality of life," the curriculum will address cultural, social, and economic topics and issues, an understanding of which is essential to the improvement of the quality of life on this planet. Notable among the specific topical areas the curriculum will address are culture and languages. Quality of life, in a planetary society, requires a sophisticated and sensitive understanding of other cultures and the ability to communicate across cultures. Ignorance of other societies and other ways of being human is an obstacle to peace. Knowledge of the earth's cultures and the ways of life of its many peoples is perhaps the first and fundamental form of peace knowledge. Human languages are the medium for encoding and transmitting the knowledge. Peacemaking will depend in large part on the success of education at producing truly multilingual peacemakers.

Within the global problematique, economic development and economic equity are two crucial issues that form a general category for a variety of areas of research and study dedicated to the elimination of poverty and to an equitable global development that can provide adequately for the needs of the world's people while sustaining the basic life-support system of the planet. In a peaceful order, needs will be defined by the peoples who are themselves concerned, so problems of participation in policy making should also be studied. Lack of equity and participation are the root of much global violence, conflict, and warfare.

The life-support systems of the planet will also be a central focus of the university curriculum in its study of problems related to environment, resources, and ecology. A respect for the Earth, a sense of stewardship of the planet, is to be a fundamental learning objective of the curriculum. The concept of Earth as the home of the diverse, multilingual human family and Earth as the root of all human development informs an ethic of interdependence that renounces the exploitative relationship humans have had to the planet. It recasts the human role as that of functioning as an integral part, rather than the master, of the ecology of Planet Earth.

Since the cultural, economic, and environmental aspects of the curriculum derive from the basic purposes of the university, it is necessary to include in the course of study issues of values, ethics, and aesthetics. An exploration of the philosophical and ethical bases of the world's cultures and political systems, an understanding of the world's religious traditions, and a sensitivity to and appreciation of the aesthetic achievements of these cultures and traditions are, we assume, essential to developing a full set of what might be called peace values. Certainly, the understanding of multiple value systems is central to cross-cultural understanding and an understanding of the true nature of human problems.

The development of a "just and peaceful planetary social order," of course, requires knowledge and understanding of comparative and conflicting values as much as knowledge of political and organizational concepts, systems, and structures. Under this general rubric, the curriculum intends to address such topics as that of conflict and its various dimensions, including conflict resolution and a whole range of conflict-resolving skills. The curriculum will also address techniques, both human and technical, of communication and of information management. It will, of course, deal with the major political issues and problems of the world social order. Such questions as the problems and violations of human rights, questions of national and international security, peace-keeping, and, most specifically, disarmament and the means to control and eliminate the arms race will be central to this aspect of the curriculum. This area of the curriculum reflects the assumption that there must be an intentional and explicit education for global citizenship. Thus, global civic education will be a central topic for the curriculum. The general notions of global citizenship that infuse most peace and global education will have to be refined into a particular set of skills and body of knowledge required for such civic responsibility.

The University for Peace seeks to develop a curriculum that can respond to the rapid changes and developments in world society and to the myriad causes of conflict in both the fundamental aspects that lie within the world system and the mind set that produces it, and in the immediate aspects that give rise to particular wars and other armed conflicts. It also must be sensitive to the fact that these conflicts are going to be viewed very differently by the various parties involved and still differently by the observers, depending upon the ideological, political, and geographic and cultural frameworks they bring to the viewing of the problems. Thus, a general principle of the university curriculum is that it must be derived from interdisciplinary, multicultural, and multi-ideological bases. The University for Peace will have to pursue an authentic world curriculum for global responsibility.

Fleshing Out the Outline: The Juniata Process

These efforts of the University for Peace might be considered as the first stages in a transnational process, which was first seriously addressed in the United States in a consultation organized in June 1986 by the Peace Studies Program of Juniata College in Huntingdon, Pennsylvania, in conjunction with the Peacemaking in Education Program of United Ministries in Education and the Teachers College Peace Education Program. The Juniata Process included consideration of resources needed for and available to peace studies; vocations, including the purposes for which peace studies attempts to educate; and rubrics, or conceptual bases, of the field. Although set in the context of university peace studies, the report of the meeting (published in the December 1986 *COPRED Peace Chronicle*), like the curriculum outline of the University for Peace, provides useful guidelines for a comprehensive program of peace education. The intention of the report, like that of this book, is to encourage a deeper and farther-ranging discussion on the substance and purposes of peace studies. The following extracts from the Juniata report represent what one group of experienced peace educators offered as a preliminary statement of a conceptual framework for peace studies.

Central proposition (i.e., major assumptions underlying most peace studies programs and curricula). The generally held, traditional belief in the inevitability of war and oppression is now called into question by data and insights derived by peace research and popular movements for human social transformation. Peace studies is mainly comprised of an examination of the traditional belief and the study and critique of the data and insights from peace research and relevant social movements. The major pedagogical purpose of the field is to challenge the traditional belief and to inquire into possibilities for alternatives to war and oppression.

As a field of inquiry, peace studies were reviewed as to the fundamental core essential to all programs and curricula; the dimensions and characteristics which vary according to approaches to the inquiry; the methodologies and theories employed; the skills and learning objectives to be pursued.

   I. The Fundamental Core (essential substance of peace studies)
      A. Central Questions of the General Inquiry
         1. What is the nature of peace?
         2. What are the conditions that make peace possible?
         3. How are these conditions achieved?
      B. Minimum Areas of Inquiry

   1. Organized lethal violence among social groups at all levels of organization (war)
   2. Structural violence (systematic discrimination, deprivation, and oppression)
 C. Basic Values
   1. A worldwide human perspective
   2. The desirability of achieving peace and justice
   3. Recognition of the *possibility* of achieving peace and justice.
. . . .
IV. Learning Objectives Pursued by Peace Studies
 A. Values and normative goals are explicit in most peace studies programs. Among those most frequently and explicitly cited are:
   1. The five "world order values": peace, social justice, economic equity, ecological balance, and political participation.
   2. Individual and personal attributes and capacities as identified in the "Vocations" section of the Juniata report.
 B. Skills are the most emphasized learning objectives in peace studies.
   1. Social Science skills are among those most widely and intentionally sought, i.e., descriptive, comparative, analytic, etc.
   2. World Order Learning Objectives are also frequently noted, i.e., creating and identifying alternatives; evaluation of policies and theories; prescription, policy and strategy formulation; action and advocacy.
   3. Some programs also cite the competencies for global peacemaking, i.e., cross cultural understanding; communications capacity; conflict recognition and resolution skills. ("Juniata Consultation," 1986)

All three of the content proposals offered here — the World Core Curriculum, the Juniata report, and the University for Peace curriculum — provide conceptual frameworks that I see as essential to comprehensive peace education. All three represent attempts to formulate a transformational approach and provide appropriate bases for the discussion of what should constitute the parameters of the field. Indeed, these outlines may well be adequate if we restrict ourselves to the field of peace *studies*, but if we deal instead with peace *education*, where the emphasis is on learning and the inner process of change, rather than on outer structural reconstruction, much more must be considered. Peace education should be as much concerned with the structures of consciousness as with the structures of society, as much with the limits to human thinking as with the limits to the fulfillment of human needs. Peace education should thus be as much concerned with context as with content.

The Notion of Paradigm Shift: A Transformational Context

Many forms of peace education seek to be, in practice and consequence, vehicles for global transformation, which implies change of the widest possible breadth in social organization and the greatest possible depth in personal perspectives and behaviors. As the overarching expression of both the learning and social purposes of peace education, paradigm shift will not be possible without the comprehensive kind of learning program outlined in Muller's World Core Curriculum and the Juniata report. It requires a historic perspective that digs deeply into the past and projects an evolution far into the future.

Indeed, the struggle for peace in its most comprehensive sense is likely to have a place on the human agenda for as many generations into the future as we can imagine. Education for peace is education for the long haul, for ongoing struggle. Educators in general are people who deal with the long haul, and education is certainly a delayed-gratification kind of enterprise. I think of this ongoing struggle from the perspectives of a teacher, a program developer, and a peace educator. For many years, my perspective was that of a classroom teacher, a practitioner. From this perspective the long haul was the future of the students, and the purpose of education was to prepare them for it. Goal achievement, in this context, certainly called for an incremental perspective. My work in program development with the Institute for World Order brought with it the opportunity to reflect, speak, and write about the questions, and my perspective became that of a theorist. From this perspective the ongoing struggle emphasizes the possibilities for developing a long-range, future-directed, globally oriented form of instruction. Goal achievement required a systems perspective.

As I became aware of the deeper issues involved in problems of peace and justice, my perspective became that of a peace educator. The central issue then was, How can this form of instruction help to achieve peace? This question produced a shift in emphasis from instructing — imparting particular knowledge — to educating, which includes both the learning that educators elicit from students and the learning that educators themselves experience in that process. As I have described elsewhere in greater detail (Reardon, in press), I came to see that the essence of this long struggle was itself a learning process, one involving individual learners, societies, the whole human species. This in turn led me to recognize a new way of conceiving the process of learning to make peace, based on the perspective of what I have termed the *edu-learner*. An edu-learner is a practitioner/theorist whose primary activity is learning while trying to help other people learn. This is the perspective that I now struggle to develop.

In fact, all able, responsible teachers are probably striving to be edu-learners. Process-centered practitioners who apply, adapt, and develop educational theory as they attempt to facilitate learning, whether in nursery school or graduate school, probably all hold this vision. Edu-learning is process-centered teaching and learning. It is purposeful and value-oriented. Education, in this sense, is preparation for participation in processes: in personal processes; interpersonal processes; social, structural, political, and, most important, ongoing learning processes. The primary function of education is to help people in doing, acting, and becoming, all of which have transformational dimensions. The most fundamental aspect of the edu-learning process is the role of the teacher as learner and the view of learning as a lifelong process of experience reflected upon and integrated into new learning in an organic, cyclical mode, a mode that is conscious of the relations between the inner experience and the outer realities.

Like many others I have spent a lot of time in peace education, as in other forms of education, trying to figure out what is it that people need to know to be peacemakers, to contribute to the achievement and maintenance of peace. The realities of any area in which we try to educate, be it society, the sciences, or the arts, are so complex and change so rapidly that we must continually redefine many of our specific educational objectives, and so we should. The process of redefinition or updating the field is as important to peace education as to any endeavor. The complexity of the present problematic world realities and the difficulties of the struggle for a transformed reality make it important that process, rather than objectives, become the paramount mode and form for education — at the very least for peace education, which aspires to be transformational. A transformational context, then, is one that pursues process learning within a consciousness of ever-expanding spheres of complexity and constant change.

Three learning processes seem to me especially helpful in striving for transformation. (There are others, some discussed in other sections of this volume, but these three are especially rich in potential.) The three, all fundamental to a deeply reflective approach that links the inner learning experience to the outer realities or learning occasions, are speculation, evaluation, and integration. *Speculation* is the capacity that enables us to bring to consciousness possibilities for new realities, the images of a transformed world. *Evaluation* is the capacity to examine and assess those and other possibilities, the multiple alternatives resulting from our own speculations and those of others, some of them perhaps in the form of world order models. *Integration* is taking the conclusions of those assessments and making them part of our cognitive systems, part of our standard learning equipment as we continue to speculate and become aware of the links between our consciousness of what we value and how that affects the social reality of the world. As we do this individually, we are engaging in process learning, in changing ourselves. The process becomes socially and politically relevant when we begin to share it, when we articulate our speculations and evaluations.

Thus dialogue and conversation are important ways to share and test learning and also to connect personal, individual change to social and political change. The dialogic mode, as noted, has been important in the political areas of peace education, especially with reference to economic structures (Freire, 1973). In my view dialogue, however, is far less transformative than conversation. Dialogue implies two parties and often falls into a pattern of the questioner and the questioned, the teacher and the learner. Partial as I am to the Socratic method, it now seems to me (and to many of my students as well) to be too teacher-centered. Conversation, on the other hand, connotes a community of inquirers, sharing questions and insights, mutually responsible for creating the knowledge necessary to the changes our common values impel us to seek. Perfecting the art of conversation as a learning mode is truly a challenge to teachers seeking to be edu-learners. The conversational mode must be developed in coordination with changes in the social and human relations within our educational institutions.

For example, we need to change the communication mode—that is, the language and the context in which we hold these conversations. Our current language is primarily conditioned by the dualistic, reductionist paradigm at the base of the war system, the competitive, conflictual core of our society that reduces most major issues to two opposing sides. In other words, the structures in which conversation takes place are conditioned by the very paradigm we are trying to transcend. In educational terms, the present paradigm focuses on specific substantive knowledge, particular skills, and varying forms of technical proficiency. Even the humanistic dimensions of education, the values found in social education, and the humane attitudes emphasized in peace education are not adequate to balance this emphasis on technical proficiency, which reinforces and maintains the dominant paradigm. As I shall assert in more detail later, peace education needs to move from *skills* development to *capacity* development, to the enhancement of *quality* rather than *quantity*, as the major measure of educational achievement. Communication, especially conversation, is a capacity, which needs to be developed as both a learning mode and a peacemaking process. We have a capacity to exchange relevant concepts, information, and, more important, values and visions, but the dominant mode of contemporary education impedes this mode (Sloan, 1984). Present educational structures and practices that reflect the values of the dominant paradigm are a serious obstacle to the development of the fundamental human capacities for peacemaking.

Capacities are like buds within us, and they blossom through our experience with others, through social and personal interactions. Through process learning, we can deepen and extend those of our human capacities that relate to changing and creating paradigms, particularly the essential transformative and creative capacities of insight and imagination (Sloan, 1984). Three creative capacities of particular importance to insight and imagination are *envisioning*, *imaging*, and *making metaphors*.

Every paradigm comes from, or at least is informed by, a vision that embodies the highest values of the paradigm. These visions are articulated by religious and political prophets, poets, artists of all kinds, philosophers, and scholars. The great religions and the major historic movements and ideologies have been based on visions that embody such values, as well as on the images or pictures in our minds of the structures and processes for realizing the values. These images determine our social norms and our political and economic systems. Metaphors are probably our most significant mode of thinking about the human experience. As we have to begin to deliberately develop capacities for envisioning and imaging, so, too, we need to develop the capacity of making new metaphors. If we seek transformation, we may have to learn to become our own prophets. We have to be able to design our own preferred reality, to make images of new social structures informed by our highest values. And we have to communicate our visions and images to others. Thus the development of the capacity for reflective, imaginative conversation is central to paradigm change and therefore to peace education. It is only through such conversation that we can create new metaphors.

Perhaps even more than images of a peaceful society, peace education needs new metaphors through which we can find the meaning of human experience and human struggle. We urgently need new metaphors if we are to transcend the war system through which society enacts the values and images of the present paradigm. The war system is not only organized warfare and armed conflict — it is all of the practices, institutions, and interrelationships that are essentially violent, that destroy relationships, that impede social development and human fulfillment. It is at the very core of our thinking and our relationships (Reardon, 1985). Yet in the midst of this war system, there is, as well, a peace system. Just as the capacity for war and violence is within us and the way we think, so too is the capacity for peace. Perhaps peace is not so much to be achieved as it is to be discovered, nurtured, and developed, as are all human capacities. In order for us to do this, we have to believe it is there within us and to know that it has existed in human experience — perhaps in long-gone times and distant places, but it has existed. We have to believe that peace is possible.

The trouble with the peace system is that few human beings have paid any attention to it. Most of us have not focused on it. Indeed, we have suppressed it. We have done to the peace system pretty much what we have done to women, women's roles, and to the feminine in all of us. We have ignored it, and when it rears its interesting head, we have suppressed it. Neither peace nor feminine qualities are valued by the Western, industrial paradigm that operates throughout the world. The war system is thus a powerful influence on the human mind. There are certain characteristics of the way in which we think that can be described as "war thinking," characteristics that can be changed, through process learning in a transformational context, to an alternative paradigm of "peace thinking." War-system thinking is dualistic; an alternative would help us to think in terms of both unity and multiplicity. War system thinking is antagonistic and confrontational; the alternative would lead us to think in terms of mutuality and negotiated consensus. The war system causes us to think in terms of ends and goals; an alternative would help us think in terms of means and processes. The dominant paradigm emphasizes analysis, pulling things apart to understand them; an alternative one would emphasize synthesis, putting things together in positive relationships. The present paradigm tends to be reductionistic, to see specific parts, to specialize knowledge and experience; an alternative would prefer holism, asserting that you cannot understand the part unless you see it in the context of the whole. This holism is necessary to thinking in terms of "organic peace" or a peace system. It is, we are told by feminists, a drastically different way of knowing than the oppositional, dualistic thinking of the patriarchy that characterizes the present paradigm.

Yet these primarily cognitive characteristics just listed are not nearly as important as the major affective characteristics of the present paradigm. Rooted in war, domination, and violence, it brings forth our capacity to mourn, more than our capacity to celebrate. We spend so much time mourning, not only the losses of war and deprivation but also our own sins, our own mistakes, which we usually see as the causes of war and violence, that we do not have time enough to celebrate our achievements, the wonderful things that we do have, are, and can become. We need to focus on our capacities to create and to celebrate. Peace education does not need to destroy the dominant paradigm so much as to ignore it for a while as we concentrate on our capacity to recognize and nurture peace.

One way is to begin to put more emphasis on life. The present paradigm has life and death out of balance. We human beings have spent so much energy and used our wits (particularly in American society) postponing and preventing death—that is our own deaths—to the point that we are quite willing to plan and bring about the deaths of others so that *we* will not die. There is much talk about the denial of death in Western culture. However, the situation may in fact be the reverse: preoccupation with death and denial of life. We have not fully explored nor left ourselves open to all the possibilities of life and this is probably why we cannot perceive the peace paradigm. Jeremy Rifkin, in *Declaration of a Heretic* (1985), deals with this phenomenon, arguing that we have focused so entirely on our security needs that they have become destructively dominant in the human experience. Indeed, the present paradigm is very security/defense oriented. Most peace studies, at least at the university level, reflect this orientation, as did the primacy of negative peace in earlier phases of peace research. Peace education must present an alternative paradigm, focused on human fulfillment and social development. Instead of spending so much of our time and treasure in trying to prevent our own deaths by preparing for the deaths of our adversaries, we could spend a lot more time and effort on maintaining and nurturing life and learning to transform adversarial relationships into complementary, cooperative ones.

We need only to look at the priorities in our national budget to see that our attention now is on security, not human needs—security in the sense of protection or defense, not security in the broader sense of the fulfillment of needs. That national priority also comes from the way we think and is clearly reflected in the way we speak and write, even in peace and feminist literature and discourse. Our language is rife with the terminology of war and violent struggle. Think only of such phrases as the "fight for peace," "ammunition for peacemakers," "target groups," and so forth. A transformative peace education would be as sensitive to militarist language as current peace education is to sexist and racist language (Leaven, 1985). Transformation requires that we change our language, as well as—or perhaps as a means to—change our way of thinking.

Most of all, we have to change our major metaphor. The prevailing metaphor for human struggle, achievement, and transcendence—warfare—emerging from patriarchy, might well be changed to the metaphor of labor and birth, human development and maturation, emerging from a more fully human, androgynous paradigm. If we begin to think primarily in terms of something as all-encompassing, as process-oriented as birth and life cycles, beginning with notions of conception, gestation, labor, bringing forth, nursing, and parenting to maturation, we could have an entirely different way of thinking and speaking about the human experience and the challenges that face us. This alternative metaphor is a comprehensive and inclusive one; it would not exclude men, as the warfare metaphor has excluded women. It is equally relevant to all cultures, ideologies, and stages of development. Nor is it biased toward the technologically dominant areas of the world. Such a metaphor also might enable us to think of process itself as an alternate purpose or goal. We would not be so preoccupied with achieving goals and winning victories. We would be thinking in terms of the long-range health and welfare of living beings.

Among the myriad possibilities for change offered by this metaphor, there are many beyond the shift from the time-bound, goal-oriented kind of thinking that could help us create a cyclical, process kind of thinking. Encounters with "others"—strangers, or people who are culturally or ideologically different—instead of causing conflict and responses of fear and antagonism, might be used instead for exploring complementarity and mutuality, looking for commonality rather than trying to defend ourselves against the other. The emphasis might shift from exclusion to inclusion; from competition to cooperation; from repressing the other to letting the other be born and fulfilled, even the "other" within each of us. From "fighting against" opponents we might move to the notion of "struggling with" them to bring forth a new relationship, as women in labor struggle together with the infant to bring forth new life. From an order of hierarchically structured sovereign states as the main notion of the way we organize global society, we might come to concepts based upon patterns of participatory interdependence and familial kinship. Both of these metaphors involve risks. In the war metaphor, as we struggle for conquest and glory, we risk mutilation, destruction, and death. Yet even today, death is risked in bringing forth life, particularly for many women in impoverished areas of the world. But that risk is the risk of life, a risk that challenges us to transcend our overwhelming preoccupation with preventing death, to shift our struggle to the enhancement of life and the fulfillment of the possibilities it offers.

Peace education should be directed not only toward the maturation of the individual but toward the coming of age of the human species. The primary indicator of such development will be the withering away of violence, as persons, nations, and the international system develop their peacemaking capacities. This coming of age is the authentic transformation, the actual paradigm shift. The context for peace education should be one of a conscious struggle to bring forth a new mode of thinking that is life-affirming, oriented toward the fulfillment of the human potential, and directed to the achievement of maturation as the ultimate goal of organic or positive peace.

CHAPTER 5

The Fundamental Purposes of a Pedagogy of Peace

Peace education, like most educational fields, aspires to excellence. If excellence, as the *Oxford English Dictionary* indicates, is the "possession of . . . good qualities in an eminent or unusual degree," the good qualities needed, I would argue, are those that would come closest to the current concept of the "positive human potential." Efforts to fulfill this human potential for authentic excellence would be a major animating force of the peace paradigm basic to the transformational approach. And although contemporary education seems very much preoccupied with excellence in the sense of preparation and capacity to compete, it seems to have little concern with qualities; it is so much obsessed (as is the competitive mode) with quantity and measurement that it is an impediment to transformation rather than a means to it.

Education should be devoted to the development of the ability to learn and should concern itself with deepening and extending the capacities that are comprehended by the notion of the positive human potential. Positive peace and the positive human potential are inextricably linked; both are developmental and organic. Many peace educators and activists would define peacemaking as conceiving, gestating, and nurturing those conditions in which all can develop their good qualities, their capacity to be fully human. Education today is not really living up to its potential. My own experience and my own activities have been, it seems to me now, more often focused on instrumental than on fundamental purposes. Much of my work—indeed the dissertation on which this volume is based—emphasized conceptualizing and designing curricula for particular learning objectives derived from earlier work (Reardon, 1981, 1982) that now appear to me to be quite limited.

Many of us continue to engage in an educative process that is much more a matter of the teacher's transmitting information or interpretations to students than a process of mutual exchange. We set our tasks too much in terms of achieving "objectives"—not only the much-maligned "behavioral objectives," but all the narrow learning goals from which we develop our curricula. When we measure our professional success, we assess our achievements by quantifying them. There is certainly a role for quantification, as there is a role for specific objectives, even behavioral objectives, in a comprehensive program for peace education. But we have placed so much emphasis on these aspects, that we have held back the possibility for developing a broader range of human capacities. For example, we put a great deal of emphasis on developing the skills of analysis, a very important set of skills. But when it becomes the dominant mode for our teaching and learning, analysis alone tends to reduce knowledge into small, isolated components. It fragments our learning and our thinking, and thereby our lives. Goals and objectives, without a larger value framework, do the same.

Goals are desired states that we work to achieve. *Objectives* are intervening points along the way, partial achievements. Because neither *goal* nor *objective* is broad enough, and neither seems to encompass the aspects of process and complexity that are so important to the field, I use the term *purpose* to describe the intentional ends of peace education. Purpose seems to connote continued pursuit of a value or good. The concept of purpose provides the larger value framework and pushes us to less instrumental thinking.

Peace educators might well review the preamble to the charter of the United Nations Educational, Social, and Cultural Organization (UNESCO), which states that "since wars begin in the minds of men, it is in the minds of men that the foundations of peace must be constructed." Putting aside a temptation to make a feminist comment on the wording, I must agree that wars begin in the minds of men — indeed, in *all human minds* — and that it is in all our minds that the foundations for peace must be constructed. If we are to be peacemakers, then we must learn to be peace thinkers. We must pursue that change in our thinking that Einstein exhorted us to seek.

If we take seriously the need to change our way of thinking, then we have to look toward the reintroduction of qualities and capacities into the educational pursuit. As Douglas Sloan has suggested, in the introduction to a special issue of the *Teachers College Record* on peace education, "A change in our way of thinking would, if nothing else, recognize and re-orient itself, in method and substance, around the *reality of qualities*. . . . The qualitative enhancement of life and of culture would become more important than their quantitative manipulation and control" (Sloan, 1982, p. 11). He argues that pursuit of quality should be at the very center of education. I would add that developing our capacities for peacemaking should also be at the very center of education, for practical as well as moral reasons. Given the complexity and dynamism of our world, continuing to educate for manipulation and control—in other words, primarily for the development of quantifiable skills—is only going to exacerbate the problems of war and violence. Emphasis on control and manipulation tends to increase violence, and so, too, it may be argued, does quantification. As Kenneth Boulding states, "Every time we count, we are doing violence to reality, for counting assumes that every item we count is the same" (Boulding, 1985).

The Centrality of Wholeness, Integrity, Complexity, and Change

Current peace education, as I have admitted, seems as much concerned with narrowly defined instruction as with authentic learning— more with the transmission of specific categories and quantities of knowledge than with the development of the capacity to learn, to change, and to transform ourselves, in order to transform our reality. If, indeed, excellence is comprised of qualities, then it is learning rather than instruction that should be the central concern of peace education. Of all education, peace education obviously needs to be primarily concerned with calling forth human capacities for excellence, most of all the capacities for peacemaking. An education that is concerned more with instruction than with learning, with quantity more than quality, is especially lamentable at this particular time in our history, when we are on the point of a possible quantum leap toward a significant new stage in the human experience, a coming of age of the human species and of human society: and the achievement of positive peace. The capacity and inclination to make peace, to bring about a nonviolent and just social order on this planet, would be the primary indicator of a maturing of our species. This quantum leap is, I believe, currently being impelled by a slowly but definitely emerging paradigm shift from an antagonistic, simplified, fragmented, reductionist view of the world, which now conditions our behaviors and institutions, to a complex, integrated, and holistic view of the world and of human society. This paradigm shift, which has been emerging in large part from new developments in physics and the convergence of physics and theology (Augros & Stanciu, 1984), must become an integral part of the way in which we approach education. It certainly is essential if education is to contribute to the development of our capacities for peacemaking, which is the central purpose of a pedagogy of peace.

Here peacemaking is construed as a dynamic, active process, and peace connotes a condition in which justice can be pursued without violence. That pursuit involves ongoing individual and social processes. Peace can come about only by an intentional, organic process of continuous change, day by day and habit by habit, as well as norm by norm and structure by structure, evolving not as much sequentially and incrementally as simultaneously and constantly. Peace is not an end state or a final goal. It is something that will have to be redefined as we continue to pursue it. Peacemaking, then, requires education for complexity; for qualities rather than quantities; for diversity; and above all, since we live in a complex and diverse world, for finding ways of making sense of it, for putting the bits and pieces together, and in so doing, for finding meaning in the experience. Meaning cannot be found in particular attitudes acquired and fixed or in specific skills mastered and applied in a sequentially time-bound sequence, nor tested by quantified measurements associated with many of our specified learning objectives, disassociated from the larger purposes of interpretation and transformation of the human condition. Meaning, it seems, can be found only in a context of integrity and wholeness, the most appropriate context for understanding complexity and making meaning out of experience.

One element of the paradigm shift to be accounted for in identifying purposes and creating contexts for peace education is this element of complexity and constant change. Education has not only been instructional; it has been directed toward specific end states, fixed in time and space in a way that attends hardly at all to change. Whether those end states be professions, trades, or permanent mind-sets, unchanging value structures or a specific set of skills to be mastered, education has been primarily about achieving end states. Many of us who work in curriculum development have designed our work around learning objectives, goals that will be achieved, left behind, or incorporated into other end-state goals. We look at education as a job to be done and finished, discrete task by discrete task, segment by segment, grade level by grade level, subject matter by subject matter, in a sequential and separated manner. Education, like our entire life itself, is largely fragmented, fractionated, and quantitatively time-bound. Peace education, however, needs to recognize, in the words of the economist Orio Giarini, that "complexity, vulnerability, uncertainty and real time [a continual flow, constant change] are becoming the operating conditions of the will to be and become" (Giarini, 1985, p. 7). These are not conditions that can be adequately met by an education dealing with end states and behavioral learning objectives. They are conditions that call on us to recognize that it is the becoming that is the significant part of being; that learning is living — not just preparation for life; that people as well as society and the natural order, are in constant change; and that a significant element of the human potential is the ability to direct the change in self and in society toward preferred values and to relate responsibly to changes in the natural order.

Peacemaking is also about becoming — individuals becoming peacemakers, society becoming peaceful, and the natural order becoming what nature ordains, being left in that state of organic peace that enables it to sustain healthy persons and creative societies. "Health" here is conceived as that state of well-being that generates a struggle to become fully human, not merely to strive to compete. It is not surprising, then, that a violent society exists simultaneously with a society and an education little concerned with health. Violence, as I previously defined it, is the intentional, avoidable doing of harm. That which is harmed is injured or ill. Indeed, violence has been described as social pathology, and violent behaviors have often been considered symptoms of mental illness. When that behavior is exhibited by nation-states, however, the symptoms are read as having "natural" causes, such as "defense of one's own interests" or "deterrence" of injury by others whose interests are seen as potentially harmful to one's own. Some scholars have seen such national policies as a form of pathology (Frank, 1962; Johansen, 1978). We live in a sick society, and education has not escaped the illness. Education has been so much concerned with producing skillful persons, productive persons, that the notion of "person" itself has come to be thought of as the recipient of training for productivity and skill development. Little concern and attention is given to health and wholeness, to integrity, either of persons or of society. Integrity is a value to which we give much lip service, usually thinking of it as meaning simply honesty or dependability and of people with integrity as those who present themselves for what they are. Yet the *Oxford English Dictionary* tells us that integrity means "unbroken wholeness without unnecessary division." I would also suggest that it means being "in harmony with a larger wholeness"; that human integrity in individual persons is related to and part of a social integrity that would permit us to live without doing violence to each other, to other groups, or to our environment, our parent planet.

There is some discussion today of education of the "whole person," or developing the various talents and abilities of the individual. Education of the whole person, however, except in some Montessori and Rudolf Steiner schools, does not usually concern itself with interconnections and interrelationships, the connections of person-to-person and of persons to the larger society and the natural environment. Education, without careful consideration of the interrelationships and integration of all levels of social organization and the natural environment as the context for the development of the human person, cannot educate for true integrity, and certainly not for authentic wholeness.

The kind of wholeness implied here requires that integrity becomes a major educational goal; certainly integrity in the traditional sense, but, most important, integrity also in the sense of wholeness and relationship to others, to society, and to the natural order. This holism is what I mean in advocating an integrated conceptual base for comprehensive peace education. Integrity as an educational goal calls for peace education to be grounded in the three comprehensive core values that I have termed *planetary stewardship, global citizenship*, and *humane relationship*. These values consistently emerged as the heart of the educational purposes of the curricula submitted to the World Policy Institute survey. I sensed in this a recognition on the part of peace educators of the centrality of wholeness and integrity to peacemaking capacities (Reardon, 1988).

The value of *stewardship* calls on us to foster in our students a consciousness of their relationship to the whole natural order and their responsibility to assure the health, the survival, and the integrity of the planet. It calls upon us to recognize our physical as well as our ethical relationship to our planet home, so that Earth itself and the integrity of Earth is the fundamental and central value of all education, but most particularly of peace education.

The value of *citizenship* calls on us to educate people to be capable of creating a nonviolent, just social order on this planet, a global civic order offering equity to all Earth's people, offering protection for universal human rights, providing for the resolution of conflict by nonviolent means, and assuring respect for the planet that produces the life and the well-being of its people.

The value of *humane relationship* is one that recognizes the interconnections and interrelationships that make up the web of life, starting with the interconnections between the human order and the natural order and emphasizing a human order of positive human relationships, relationships that make it possible for all to pursue the realization of individual and communal human potential. The creation of positive human relationships is the task of peacemaking, and preparation for positive human relationships should be an overarching purpose of education. Such positive relationships would require, at a minimum, the rejection of those forms of organized violence that prevent the achievement of negative peace and would intensify social efforts to transcend the structural violence that impedes the realization of positive peace.

Impediments to Transformation

In order to achieve these goals, we must nurture a range of peacemaking capacities central to the process of maturation. Such capacities would enable us to transcend the tendencies that currently characterize both education and our social order. The negative characteristics of the reductionist paradigm that I have identified in Chapter 4 as the major obstacle to the transformative context sought by peace education are the seven negative *R*s of *resignation, repression, reduction, rejection, redress, retribution*, and *reservation*. These characteristics are paramount in all our relationships and affect our modes of teaching. We are *resigned* to a limited potential for individuals and for society, specified by "intelligence quotients" and "planning projections." We have *repressed* possibilities for wider horizons, for capacities we designate as "primitive" or "nonrational." Modes of knowing other than the scientific and analytic, such as the feminine, the intuitive, the ways of indigenous peoples, have been greatly undervalued by our educational institutions. We have *reduced* the rich complexity of the whole of the world and what we know of it to the simplest components, isolated from one another in separate disciplines and subjects, arranged hierarchically and taught sequentially in grade order and in order of "significance" — that is, of instrumental value. We have *rejected* the challenges to the prevailing paradigm that have come from sources identified as not suitable for holding authority — from women, from traditional societies, from nonwhite peoples — and even from those who use the very tools of the prevailing paradigm to question its assumption and values. We have sought to *redress* with negative means challenges and violations of our notions of what is valuable and appropriate. We hold a notion of justice that is at best compensatory and at worst retaliatory. We seek *retribution* from those who challenge, from those who upset our notions of what is right and orthodox, as well as those who threaten or harm us. Our society continues to consign to lesser humanity those of different political persuasion, as well as those of other races and cultures, and "the second sex," women.

Perhaps most destructive of all, we hold ourselves in *reserve* from others and from the very living system that has given us our own lives. We seek "objective" knowledge at the sake of "subjective" truth. The consequences of this separation of the knower from the known have probably been the real root causes of that whole array of planetary crises that comprise the global problematique in the curriculum framework of the University for Peace described in Chapter 4. Reliance on observation and analysis as the dominant way of knowing has helped to sustain the war system and has prevented us from taking advantage of many other ways of knowing. Now, as feminists bring to our attention what we have lost in devaluing women's ways of knowing (Belenky et al., 1986), we need to be especially sensitive to this tendency to separate and hold ourselves in reserve from others, their suffering and their capacities, and from all the rich possibilities of a complex, multidimensional, organic, human relationship to the living planet Earth. We must learn to see ourselves as a part of, not apart from, our planet and all of its inhabitants.

Since negative peace involves the dismantling of the war system, the transcendence of violence, and the undoing of patterns of behavior made possible by war and violence, so a pedagogy of peace needs to be about undoing and transcending these characteristics of the reductionist paradigm. However, undoing them certainly should not be the center of pedagogical purposes. Indeed, it seems that much of peace education (as noted in Chapter 2) has been more concerned with teaching people about the danger of these negative characteristics than with transcending them. Overconcentration on the negative also seems to have affected many peace movements, so that they are themselves fragmented, some even alienated from the living Earth. In seeking to reverse these negative characteristics and conditions, they use some of the very behaviors and processes that these characteristics have created. Thus, even some peace education exemplifies the prevailing paradigm, reifying the present system, which pursues stability rather than struggle for true equity; seeks simplicity rather than accept complexity; and grabs at certainty rather than confront ambiguity. We peace educators, too, have often educated toward limited learning objectives, end states, specific skills, and given knowledge content. Not all peace studies have been presented or pursued in a positive, peacemaking way.

Peacemaking Capacities: Generalized Learning Purposes

As the essential learning purposes of comprehensive peace education I would emphasize the development of seven essential capacities for peacemaking, or seven fundamental *R*s of peace education. These fundamental capacities, which I see as the antithesis of the negative *R*s that impede transformation, are *reflection, responsibility, risk, reconciliation, recovery, reconstruction*, and *reverence*. All of these belong to the realm of quality rather than quantity. They are elements to be called forth from each learner and nurtured through a holistic form of education that cannot be limited to the achievement of specific objectives or quantifiable goals.

Reflection is something to which we give little time in our educational schedules. The social educator, Lawrence Metcalf, and his colleague Maurice Hunt elaborated processes for developing "reflective thinking" as the requisite mode of social education (Hunt & Metcalf, 1955). Reflection, they say, "refers to the essential but non-gadget-like features of the scientific method" (p. 59). This mode of thinking, basically a reasoning process, is certainly necessary to prepare people for participation in a democratic political order and for sound decision making. Reflective thinking, however, although an essential and fundamental component, is only part of what is meant here by reflection. We need to encourage a type of reflectiveness that permits us to look beyond our ordinary understandings of reality, to move into something approaching a meditative or contemplative process through which we deepen our understanding of personal, social, and global realities. Such a process would enable us to see things more clearly at various levels, and teach us to value silence as the occasion or "space" for reflection. It is in these reflective spaces of silence that we can most readily discover our connectedness to others and to the living Earth. Teachers will need to learn to tolerate silence in their classrooms. We will all need to learn to become more comfortable with periods of silence in our interactions as we work together in decision-making and peacemaking processes.

We need, too, to develop a capacity for another form of silence, reflective listening. This is a capacity comprised of various skills like those of concentrated attention and interpretation, which is especially needed by the most articulate among us—statesmen, teachers, and students alike. The high rewards accorded skills of verbal expression often impede the development of listening skills. Lack of these skills is, I believe, a major obstacle in many of our efforts toward peace, especially in our negotiating processes. Many of the techniques developed for business negotiation and successful group dynamics are quite relevant to peace and disarmament negotiation. They need, however, to be transposed from the win–lose to the win–win context, and beyond that to the context of deeper understanding of and interconnectedness with others.

Reflective listening skills would assure far more effective communication and would certainly enhance learning. They include the forms of affirmative, nonjudgmental listening that accord equal respect to all parties to a communication or a learning experience. They also call for full engagement to "read" all signals for the full meaning; to "interpret," or place the meaning in context; and to be critical, in the sense of looking for points of both agreement and disagreement but to do so in a manner that maintains fundamental respect for the human dignity of all, no matter how deep the disagreements are. Peacemaking can be in many ways as conflictual as war making. The adversarial modes of discourse now used in academic discussions and political debates should be replaced with transformative ones. Paramount among these modes is respectful, reflective listening. Reflection is a requirement for responsible action, both individual and social.

Responsibility is the most essential active peacemaking capacity, one that requires as preparation rational, meditative, and interpretative reflection. Active responsibility is responsibility *for* and responsibility *to*. Responsibility *for* involves acknowledging and assuming the cost of our own complicity in the violence and injustice of the war system and the values that uphold it, acknowledging that we as individuals and as a society have accepted and gone along with the systems of violence and exploitation, exploitation by the northern industrial nations of the southern, the so-called underdeveloped, poorer nations, whose poverty in large part results from our having enjoyed their resources, having access to them at less than just prices as we purchase commodities in international trade.

Responsibility *to* is a responsibility to those with whom we are inextricably interconnected in the global web of life, a responsibility for acting to change these conditions. Responsibility to the others in this world system who have been deprived of a fair share of the world's benefits calls us to critically evaluate that system and create alternatives to it. This responsibility to take action is one that involves risk.

So *risk taking*, too, is a peacemaking capacity. The capacity to take risks is the capacity to face the consequences of change, the capacity to willingly involve oneself in the process of change, changing systems and structures, changing our own circumstances within systems, structures, and relationships, and ultimately even changing the ways in which we live our lives and the ways in which we relate to others. The capacity to risk how we live and indeed how we perceive ourselves, and, in some cases, our very identities, is one of the most essential challenges to peace education. Without the capacity to risk, will we have the courage to live in new public and private realities, or will we be able to involve ourselves in creating them? For we will need to confront and resolve the conflicts that these changing realities are bound to produce, as well as the conflicts that will continue to be produced by the inequities of the present system. We must be able to work through such conflicts and reconcile the conflicting parties, all of whom are members of the human family and part of the unity of the living Earth.

Reconciliation is often recognized as a significant peacemaking capacity, yet we have not adequately addressed ourselves to developing the specific modes, behaviors, and attitudes that foster reconciliation, nor have we pursued the development of this capacity as an educational goal. We need to develop the capacity to reconcile not only the politically conflicting parties in the world but also many of the other elements now in conflictual, destructive relationship to each other—those fragmented relationships that characterize personal as well as international systems and processes.

Most especially, we will have to do some reconciling even of the parts of ourselves that we find in conflict, of the very ways in which we think. Our fragmented and adversarial patterns of thinking may well lie at the very heart of our problems of violence and injustice (Sloan, 1984). The self-healing will be as important as the healing of the society. Certainly holism and integrity cannot characterize either persons or societies developed from the reductionist thought that still dominates both our educational and our policy-making processes.

The metaphor of the "broken world" is one that pervades all aspects of the current human experience, from the planet ravished by "progress and development" and threatened with destruction by conflict and war, to personal relations and individual senses of personhood. All of life is in bits and pieces; the human family is broken and bleeding. Healing the wounds and reconciling the estranged and alienated are fundamental to the process of transition to the transformed society necessary to peace. That transformation must take place in our structures and our relationships but, most important, in the way in which we view the world and our part in our paradigm. Yet even the emergence of a holistic paradigm will not do away with the need for the capacity to reconcile. For as long as conflict and change are part of the human experience, reconciliation will be necessary to the continuation of the experience. And without the capacity to reconcile, we cannot expect to recover from the trauma of the paradigm shift essential to the change from a war system to a peace system.

Recovery—the transcending of that trauma of the excessive change and conflict of a system change, returning to health and wholeness— requires strength and a form of courage that we have not yet acknowledged as the essence of heroism. But recovery also refers to reclamation, uncovering or rediscovering, regaining that which has been lost. The regaining of much of what has been repressed and forgotten of human capacities may be essential to the transcending of the pain and shock of paradigm shift. It may indeed be the most hopeful aspect of our search to develop the capacity to recover. As indicated earlier, there is much to be recovered from our past, much that we know about how to build positive human relations and create peace. There is also much that is repressed in our images of the future. Feminist scholarship is bringing to our attention a whole realm of human experience and modes of imaging that can contribute to peacemaking (E. Boulding, 1976). Surely we have much to learn from uncovering other parts of the human experience that have been devalued or repressed in the present paradigm.

We also need to build a new reality, to reconstruct the fragments of our broken world, to bring together the positive elements that we can uncover, create, and imagine in a new paradigm of integrity and wholeness, to reconstruct a healthy, wholesome human society on the planet, to answer the call for new notions of power and courage, to put into action constructive uses of imagination that we have long neglected in our education.

The capacity for *reconstruction*, more than any other of the *R*s, involves the uses of imagination for peacemaking. The development of imaginative capacities is one of the most commonly cited purposes of peace education. It is the main purpose of several of the curricula in the K–12 curriculum guide (Reardon, 1988) and has featured in much of the theoretical literature. In terms of the capacity for reconstruction, it seems to me that there are three distinct manifestations of the imagination, which range from the deepest level of insight to the practical level of design skills.

The deepest of the three is *envisioning*, which enables us to experience insight into the full range of possibilities for realizing human potential through the expression of the most fundamental human values.

Imaging, as distinct from envisioning, is more readily integrated into conversation, particularly in the sphere of the exploration of values. Imaging is the visualization of the conditions that would prevail if those values were realized. Where visions seem to require the arts, poetry, and philosophy for expression, images can be described in the narrative of discourse.

Modeling, the most practical of the three, the closest to the sphere of skills, involves the design of social and political structures, of economic and political processes and patterns of human relationships that manifest the actual realization of the values in our lived experience. We often use models as "blueprints for preferred futures." The capacity for modeling has been significant in the reform and reconstructionist approaches to peace education. Imaging links these approaches to the transformative, which struggles with the releasing of our visionary capacities, our talents for the prophetic.

The prophetic capacity leads us to the seventh and the most comprehensive — and, I think, the most meaningful — of all the fundamental peacemaking capacities, *reverence*. (This concept is adapted from Douglas Sloan's contribution to a discussion at the Peace Education Seminar at Teachers College, Columbia University, in September 1986.) But reverence should not be ascribed only to the prophets of the great social visions nor limited to religious education. It is a universal capacity, one that our scientific paradigm has denigrated, and democracy has misinterpreted, but from which authentic joy in life can most readily spring. I use the term *reverence* to mean not only respect for truth and goodness but also the deepest appreciation of the fullness and infinite possibilities of life, possibilities that, it appears, we have experienced only in limited fashion in those centuries since we first became conscious of ourselves as human beings. Reverence is the source of wonder, which is the parent of authentic learning. Reverence is the source of our capacity to hope and the ground from which human compassion springs, the primary manifestation of the sense of connectedness and understanding of interrelationship that is at the center of the three comprehensive value goals of peace education, stewardship, relationship, and citizenship. Reverence provides the wholeness and integration of the other six capacities.

Developing educational programs to nurture these capacities is a major challenge to peace education. It calls upon us to venture into new, sometimes frightening, territory. It calls us to restructure our own professional realities. It challenges us to practice our profession in ways that we have done only in bits and pieces in the past. What Douglas Sloan (1983) has referred to as the "recovery of wholeness" will enable us to put those bits and pieces together and to imagine and create the missing pieces so that we can pursue the authentic purposes of education, the enrichment of the human experience, and strive more effectively toward the superordinate goal of peace education, assuring the continuation of the human experience by transcending the true cause of violence, alienation from life.

Teaching Toward the Development of Peacemaking Capacities

Although the classroom pursuit of the seven fundamental capacities will indeed require significant changes in educational practice, it is apparent, especially from the results of the World Policy Institute survey, that many classroom teachers are already actively engaged in teaching that reflects these purposes. The resulting curriculum guide (Reardon, 1988) contains units and teaching suggestions that are readily adaptable to the recommendations that follow. Indeed, these recommendations are largely inspired by those curricula and other current practices in peace education.

Teaching for the development of reflective capacities will require a renewed emphasis on the kind of approaches advocated by Hunt and Metcalf (1955) and by some of the discipline-based analyses of the "new social studies" approach of the sixties. In these practices, reflective thinking was an essential component of the modes of inquiry and problem solving that were widely advocated for teaching the skills essential to citizenship in a democratic society. However, new dimensions will also need to be explored. As noted earlier, the creative potential of silence has largely been overlooked. The need of all, even the youngest learners, for private time and silent spaces in which to engage in reflection has to be recognized. The meditation techniques currently being introduced into some peace education programs have great potential for the fulfillment of this need. The silence of affirmative listening and the silence of contemplative meditation both provide conditions in which reflective capacities can be developed, and both are conditions that should be encouraged in peace education classrooms.

Teaching responsibility is also teaching for empowerment. Responsibility can best be learned by taking responsibility. Students need to have the opportunity to make real choices, not simply to form opinions regarding issues — a subject of study but not of real decision making. They need opportunities to make choices that will lead to action directly related to the issues. Opportunities for individual actions and group actions to be pursued within the general community and the larger society need to be integrated into peace education curricula. Students who engage in social and political action at every age have an invaluable experience of reality that teaches the difficulties of and the possibilities for social change. They are given a sound basis on which to make judgments about social reality as well as to assess the effectiveness of their own actions. It is important that teachers communicate to students that even the most carefully chosen actions do not necessarily lead to the desired ends, that taking action is part of the ongoing process of learning to be effective change agents, of learning to refine action and to direct it more effectively toward the desired purposes. Education for empowerment, responsibility, and action is also a form of process learning. It is closely related to the cycle of reflection and action, or praxis process, integral to Paulo Freire's (1973) method of consciousness-raising for political empowerment and liberation.

Another element in teaching for responsibility is equally important: helping students to appreciate the responsibility of having and creating knowledge. This responsibility has been most discussed in the realm of the sciences, particularly as related to weapons development. However, students need to be aware that all knowledge, the derivation of knowledge and the transmission of knowledge, carries responsibilities, and that responsible learners are those who retain that sense of responsibility as they incorporate the knowledge into their own paradigms and behaviors.

The exercise of responsibility is the exercise of values reflected upon and values pursued in personal, social, and political interactions. Authentic valuing produces action and involves risks. Students can be helped to learn that risk taking is integral to commitment to values, that if we must pursue changes in order to realize our values, then risk is inevitable. Indeed, in the Freirian context, and in the experience of those who have applied it to their own liberation, risk taking is a profoundly significant part of the empowerment process. The taking of risks empowers the risk takers to take further risks and to develop the capacity to deal with the consequences of actions. It should lead to more reflection on the changed conditions, so that further action can be taken, and to an understanding that at each level new risks are likely to arise.

Risk takers are confident people, and education has not been very effective at building confidence in learners. We tend instead to undermine confidence and to teach students to avoid risk by reinforcing the social norms that encourage conformity, and we limit as we assess the potential of particular learners, by grade levels or by learning style, in quantifiable terms. We undermine confidence by using competitive grading systems and standardized curricula and teaching practices. We do not create in our classrooms a favorable climate for risk taking and confidence building. Creativity and individuality, though given much lip service, are not given much chance for development, except among those who exhibit the specific talents that the prevailing paradigm values so highly. Those whose talents lie in different areas are, too often, discouraged from exploring their talents. The competitive nature of our classrooms impedes the development of individual talents and aborts the potential for complementarity that is so important to positive peace. Rather than measuring students against each other in assessing their learning and their learning capacities, schools must help students to develop complementarities, ways in which their special talents can be integrated into communal capacities for striving toward the realization of common goals and shared values. If we are going to encourage the values of diversity and universal dignity, then variations in learning styles and approaches to problem resolution must be handled very differently in our classrooms. These variations must be looked upon as examples of the wonderful array of human potential and possibilities. Complementarity is, in essence, the core of much of what is practiced in cooperative learning (Johnson & Johnson, 1984). Much relevant work is being done in this field. Cooperative learning is certainly necessary for the development of the positive attitude toward otherness that is so important to transformational education.

Consciously nurturing positive attitudes toward otherness and human differences is fundamental to developing the capacity of reconciliation. Reconciliation, in fact, might well be pursued by having the classroom be a place for the celebration of otherness and diversity, much as is the practice in peace-related, multicultural education. Instruction needs to communicate the notion that reconciling differences does not mean eliminating them. Rather, it means accommodating to differences in a constructive and positive, and a cooperative rather than a destructive, negative, and conflictual, manner. That differences represent an exciting challenge to the integrative needs of our society, to the search for integrity and wholeness, is a concept that can be intentionally taught. Differences should be presented as the pool of possibilities for other ways of knowing and other ways of being that may help us to transform the realities of the war system. Most especially, the capacity for reconciliation must be included in education for conflict resolution. It should, perhaps, be considered both as a culminating phase and the context of conflict resolution. Not just the settlement of disputes, but the true reconciliation of the disputing parties might well be the purpose of transformative conflict-resolution processes. The notion of reconciliation and the capacity to reconcile can be integrated into much of what we now teach in world studies, in comparative systems, in the analysis of conflicting ideologies, and the problems of sexism, racism, and colonialism and world community building. Reconciliation is the manifestation of wholeness, relatedness, and integrity. Teaching for the recognition of interconnection is teaching toward reconciliation.

Recovery, both as healing and as discovery, as a concept and as a capacity, might well become a major theme in our teaching of history. The notion of recovery as healing might be illustrated as we emphasize authentic moments of reconciliation in history or instances in which destructive situations and relationships were overcome or transformed by human actions. Recovery as the discovery of human capacities practiced in our past or by those of other cultures and other places in the world can open for students a significant possibility to be hopeful and constructively idealistic. If an ideal can be found actually to have existed in our own past or in the history of other cultures, then we can be hopeful of the possibility of achieving it in our own space and time.

Recovery also calls for us to open up more possibilities for imagination and spontaneity and for a sense of adventure. If we enable students to have experiences in which they look for specific capacities and conditions in their own environments, their classrooms, schools, families, communities, and within the problems with which they actually are faced, as well as within the history they are studying, they can also become aware of their own capacities for recovery. By practical application of exercises in imaging and modeling, they can become aware of their capacities not only to mend the broken world but to rebuild and transform it.

Mending and rebuilding are essential components of the capacity for reconstruction. In some ways, the capacity for reconstruction pulls together the other five capacities, for reconstruction requires reflection on what in the reality needs to be mended and what needs to be newly created, as well as evaluation to determine what needs to be discarded. It requires

the responsibility to formulate the proposals and take the actions necessary to make the changes. It requires the risk of trying the new, the often
untried. It requires reconciling elements that have been working against
each other into a common endeavor. And it requires recovering all the
skills, all the knowledge of social planning and of creating social structures that humans have used in the past to bring about new social orders.
Such capacities can be exercised and learned by giving students opportunities to engage in actual social planning; planning the structure of their
own relationships in the classroom; planning the sequence and method of
their own curriculum, to whatever extent it is practical; and, where possible, working with outside groups that are actively involved in planning
for social change. Schools that now use their own communities as learning laboratories have shown that we already have many opportunities to
teach toward the development of these and other capacities.

Finally, teaching toward reverence can be done only in an atmos-
phere of reverence. The classroom must be a place in which mutual
human respect is the norm, in which children and learners of all ages are
valued and experience is valued. Respect for the unique gifts of each
individual, complemented by reverence for the common humanity we all
share, and joyous wonder as the stance toward life and the Earth that
sustain it, are attitudes to be manifested by teachers, nurtured in learners,
and struggled for in the consciousness of society.

Transformational Approaches to Learning

The various pedagogical purposes just discussed are largely brought
together in the capacity for reconstruction, for it is in reconstruction that
we engage in the actual transformational process. As noted earlier, world
order studies has developed reconstructive teaching practices appropriate
to comprehensive peace education. The world order method of inquiry,
although it lacks some of the important transformational components,
lends itself well to the development of essential peacemaking skills and
can be integrated into a process learning approach, if placed within the
context of a holistically oriented pedagogy. For this or any other comprehensive mode of inquiry to be truly transformational, however, it must, as
we have seen, start from a base of superordinate purposes and fundamental capacities, rather than from the present skills orientation. As an example of how such educational methods rooted in the development of specific skills might accommodate a capacity-development approach, I want
to suggest a process that is, like world order inquiry, essentially reconstructive, but that, because it is more cyclical than sequential and is not
confined to rational analysis, may have somewhat greater potential to be

transformational. I propose this process as a means to integrate my former emphasis on skills into my emerging concern with the notion of capacity development, and I offer it here as a contribution to the ongoing exploration of appropriate and effective approaches to peace education.

The educational process that currently preoccupies me is one of phases or cycles of learning experiences, composed of activities that exercise various skills (skills that I now see as components of the more general peacemaking capacities). Each cycle begins and ends with confronting reality and moves through phases, which merge one into the other, of capturing visions, formulating images, articulating preferences, constructing models, assessing possibilities, planning policies, taking action, reflecting on and evaluating change, and, again, confronting reality.

Confronting reality is essentially the kind of process that world order methodology designates as diagnosing problems and that Freire describes as the development of critical consciousness. The skills of this phase are primarily critical skills, the kinds of interpretative and analytic operations that Brookfield, in his discussion of how learners deal with the media (1986), has referred to as "deconstructing" and "decoding." A transformational process learning approach to this phase would also emphasize that the reality, and therefore the diagnosis and the interpretation, are constantly changing and are so complex that we must continually reassess the adequacy of our knowledge as we confront problems.

Because most of the present reality, viewed and assessed from the perspective of the values of peace and justice, is antithetical to human purposes and human possibilities, the imperative of change toward a preferred reality produces the next phase. The need for direction and hope brings forth the attempt to envision a transformed world. Fundamental values are identified and articulated — values of even deeper significance than the five world order values, values of the order of the affirmation of life and universal human dignity, and the three core values of stewardship, citizenship, and relationship. These are values in which the feminine capacity of sensitivity converges with the masculine values of rationality to provide a more holistic framework for formulating images of a preferred reality. This phase is one through which capacities for envisioning and speculating can be developed by the practice of the skills of meditation and reflection and by the creative and constructive uses of silence. From these visions, in which insights into fundamental and holistic value alternatives can be derived, images can be formed.

The process of formulating images develops imaginative capacities by the intentional conceptualization of alternative realities. It exercises both conceptual skills and valuational skills. As the envisioning process brings insights into an awareness of fundamental values, imaging enables us to identify and define them in descriptive terms. Defining values is necessary to articulating and determining preferences and to the formulation of policy alternatives and options for action.

In a complex and conflictual world, different value systems strenuously compete with each other. Even as more commonality of values is identified among human groups and as we seek to reconcile our values and transcend alienation, the range is still broad enough that if values are to be a unifying force in social transformation, value preferences will have to be articulated and negotiated. In the discourse that will be required to reach consensus about communal values for a transformed world society, peacemakers, if they are to communicate and defend their value preferences, will need to be skilled at reasoning and advocacy as well as at description. The articulation and selection of value preferences is the learning activity that can best be served by—and will also be most effective in developing—the capacity for conversation in which images and preferences are described, exchanged, and advocated.

Once the common preferences and values have been agreed upon, the structural and normative changes required for transformation can be conceptualized. Constructing models will require even more refined skills of specifying, analyzing, and clarifying values. It will also require the development of skills for understanding the relationships between structures and functions in the social order, as ecologists seek to understand these aspects of the natural order. Modeling will also contribute to the development of the invention and design skills that are needed for devising procedural means to achieve human purposes. Once there is a proposed alternative structure for global society that embodies the preferred common values, or, as it is described in world order literature, a "model of a transformed international system," policy planning to bring about the new system can be undertaken. Social and political action can be pursued in the light of the vision, guided by the model.

In order to move from the present reality to the preferred reality described in the model, learners require experience with planning policies. Policy planning requires skills in choosing appropriate actions for implementing values and in integrating various action plans into a general approach to realize the intention embodied in the model. When such policy plans initiate action for change, the capacity for risk and for reconstruction are also developed.

Policy planning depends upon the assessment of possibilities for change. Such assessment requires the skills of analyzing and identifying resources, as well as assessing the conflicting and common interests of the parties who need to consent to the process. This type of analysis shifts into an authentically transformational mode when learners engage in activities that allow them to develop their capacity for reconciliation, as they do when they seek to reduce conflict and enhance cooperation in using resources and pursuing of interests. Policy planning in a transformational mode brings into play the essential need to accord primacy to the interests of the entire human species as a whole and to consider as the fundamental unit of analysis the entire world system.

Assessing possibilities for change requires constant confrontation with reality and continual review of the complex and changing nature of the problems. It also provides an occasion for reminding learners of the interrelationship among different problems and the importance of basing problem-solving skills on this interrelationship. In other words, peace education should help students to confront reality, not so much problem by problem but as a set of interrelated problems presented within the context of a "problematique." The interrelationship might be articulated in the curriculum as "problem clusters"—clusters of issues, concerns, and conflicts that surround the major value issues, which are so interdependent in their causes and manifestations that their resolution cannot be sought in isolation. The notion of problem clusters also carries with it the notion of cycles and changes, as well as complexity. While inextricably interrelated, the problems also have their own respective dynamics and causes, and they may evolve at different rates and in different places. The cluster relationship can help students to see problems in a multidimensional, dynamic context. It can also help learners, as well as teachers, to appreciate the need to design learning experience that will extend and deepen their fundamental peacemaking capacities as they recognize that the resolution of complex, volatile issues calls for more than one set of problem-solving skills. Such an approach will help students to learn to understand change as a constant of life, to celebrate it as the means of widening human possibilities, and to direct it toward a more humane social order.

Although the phases outlined here are in need of testing and development, each of them is already manifest in some of the classrooms and other learning settings where education for peace is pursued. I know that practical methods for implementing process learning for transformation can be designed, because many of them already exist. Yet the task of elaborating specific methods and designing the necessary comprehensive curricular programs remains a major challenge to peace education.

CHAPTER 6

Toward Comprehensive Peace Education

Comprehensive peace education connotes a generalized approach to education for global responsibility in a planetary nuclear age; it operates at all levels and in all spheres of learning, includes all fields of relevant knowledge, and is a lifelong, continuous process. Although its general purpose can be described as education *for* peace as a transformed global social order, the learning entailed in acquiring the skills and arts of peacemaking is far more than education *about* peace. Given the breadth of the purposes of the field and the far-reaching character of the recommended content, I would argue that comprehensive peace education should be the fundamental framework for most social learning, and certainly for all formal education. In short, the basic direction for educational development should be toward embracing the possibilities of the human transformation that is both urgently needed and possible.

The Dimensions of Comprehensive Peace Education

The scope of such education cannot adequately be described in traditional curricular form. Indeed, it is, I believe, premature to undertake so specific a form of planning, though ultimately a curriculum must be systematically planned. Peace educators themselves must first engage in a transformational process, envisioning the values to be sought and imaging the educational process for which model curricula might be planned. For me, the reflections shared in this book have been a kind of preparation for envisioning and imaging. What I should like to do now is share what I see as the potential dimensions of comprehensive peace education, within which the imaging and modeling might take place.

Four essential dimensions need to be kept in mind as we begin to formulate our images. The first dimension consists of an integrated, holistic education in which the whole person, in the context of the whole planetary order, is at the center of the educational process. That process should enable the person to be actively and consciously integrated with the whole through developing an awareness of, and some degree of conscious participation in, all of the planetary systems and the various interlinkages that have been mentioned earlier.

The second dimension is the human context, particularly the points of interlinkage that bind us all together. Emphasizing these points will enable the person to see relationships among the various systems that make up the human dimensions of the global system, the economic system, the social system, the interpersonal system — and, most especially, the links between person and person, person and group, and between different groups. These relations should be seen in the context of social, economic, and political processes operating at all levels of social organization and, most important, in the context of a common struggle to transform the relations, to bring them into harmony with the whole, using as the metaphor for the whole the natural world and the harmonious ecological interrelationships of the natural world in its unmanipulated state.

The third dimension is the ecological and the planetary. A holistic vision integrating the various systems would emphasize the planet as the host of the systems and would express an ecological ethos. It would also emphasize the notions of interdependent functions and processes involving delicate natural balances that must be respected and maintained, so that the natural order, the planet home, can continue as a viable host for the human experiment.

The fourth dimension is the organic and the developmental. The learning should be seen as part of a developmental process — the development of the individual, of the human species in general, and of the species in relationship to other species and other parts of the whole, engaging in a process relationship, an organic, living process of development, in the sense of the development of an organism, a life-form. The learning should enable the learner to relate through the mind, as well as through physical relationships, to the planet and come to know those relationships as a living, interdependent reality, a planetary consciousness.

To some, these divisions may seem so broad as to be impractical. However, each is already evident to some degree in present practice, just as the specific phases of envisioning, imaging, and modeling are already exemplified in some curricula. In fact, I believe that I became aware of these dimensions because I have observed them — perhaps not all in one program, one approach, or even one articulated vision, but nevertheless visible somewhere, embedded in some practice now being used in peace education. Moreover, various practices have manifested several of the dimensions, indicating the possibility that they can be brought together in a comprehensive approach.

The Values and Qualities of Comprehensive Peace Education

Early in this book, I observed that current practice seemed to be deeply influenced by the pursuit of three superordinate values, and that those values appear in various forms throughout peace education curricula. The value concepts, which I termed *planetary stewardship, global citizenship*, and *humane relationships*, inform all of the other peace-related values, including world order values, global community values, the values expressed in human rights, ecological, and environmental movements and studies, and in all of those values that lead toward transformation.

Each of those values relates as well to various human capacities – the seven that I have stressed particularly, as well as all of the other human capacities that will be called upon as we consciously move into a transformational mode in education and social development. Continuing my earlier efforts to emphasize the importance of quality in the concept of capacity (in contrast to the more common emphasis on quantity), I want to mention certain other, general capacities that are critical for the achievement of the three central values. In a sense, these capacities comprehend and include the seven already discussed, just as the three superordinate values comprehend all the other peace values. These three human capacities, which seem almost to pair with the core values, are *care, concern*, and *commitment*.

The capacity to *care* is one for which most peace educators are now consciously trying to educate. Many educators in the humanistic tradition have worked on this concept. Some have developed significant learning and instructional procedures to develop it in learners (Laor, 1978). Care is the central quality essential to planetary stewardship. It is the comprehensive affective purpose of peace education. It requires the development of knowledge of self as knower and lover. It is coming to know what knowledge and knowing is. I was interested to hear a Jewish scholar point out, in a discussion of transformational potential, that the word *knowledge* and the term *to know* are rooted in the concept of *love*. "To know," in the biblical sense, was intended to mean "to love," "to join with," and "to care," so that this affective purpose deals with the emotional development of the person, with the capacity to establish and maintain mutually fulfilling relationships and to feel "invested" in a network of such interrelationships.

The intellectual development of the lover-knower is expressed in the overarching cognitive purpose of the development of the capacity for *concern*, the quality of concern that I would define as "attentiveness to problems—the problems of value deficits, value denials, or the violation of values." Concern is that which impels the learner to acquire information, to be "knowledgeable" about an issue or a problem. In that problems are really defined in terms of values, the quality of concern illustrates the integral relationship between the cognitive and the affective in the learning process and in the acquisition and application of knowledge.

Concern comes from information relating to issues and circumstances that we care about. Concern is developed through informed attentiveness, through disciplined focus, through various qualities and capacities that educators have long emphasized as essential to the development of the mind and the intellect, among them critical capacity. It is concern that makes for effective and active citizenship. It is concern that is at the core of the practice of citizenship in a democracy.

Effective democratic citizenship demonstrates *commitment* to the well-being of the commonweal. Commitment is the active synthesis of knowledge and value and is evidence of both the capacity for and the sense of agency on the part of the citizen-learner. Various philosophers of education have regarded this sense of agency as essential to responsible education for citizenship in a democratic society. The capacity for commitment and the sense of agency—the capacity to take action—are the fundamental rationale for teaching critical skills, for developing awareness of problems of value denial. Commitment is demonstrated by continual effort to reach value goals and continued pursuit of information in areas of concern. It is the acting-out of caring, for active commitment and social responsibility are those qualities that manifest and sustain the value of humane relationships, in the global social realm as well as the personal. It demonstrates care for those with whom we are interlinked, even when we do not directly encounter them.

There is yet a fourth quality, which I call *cohesiveness* or *cohesion*, that can be summed up in the colloquial phrase, "getting it together." This quality is the conscious attempt to integrate care, concern, and commitment—the affective, cognitive, and active. Through cohesiveness the person finds meaning in the experiences of relationships, citizenship, and stewardship; it is that which makes for personal and planetary wholeness.

Spheres of Capacity Development

The practicality of this comprehensive framework for peace education is most readily seen in its developmental and structural aspects. The development of each capacity described in this section relates directly to the realms of experience that have been used as the basic framework for the very practical peace education efforts of such programs as Leaven, described in the curriculum guide, and in the approach to peacemaking outlined in *Peacemaking Without Division: Moving Beyond Congregational Apathy and Anger*, by Patricia Washburn and Robert Gribbon (1986). These two approaches offer a framework for analysis of learning and action that has three levels: the personal, the communal interpersonal, and the global transpersonal. Because I wish to emphasize experience and learning and to avoid any hierarchical, sequential connotations, I will refer to these three as *spheres* of learning.

Developmentally, the capacity for caring centers on the person and is reflected in the individual's growth as lover and knower; it therefore corresponds to the personal sphere. The development of this capacity depends very greatly on a positive self-concept that allows one to appreciate one's own worth, special gifts, and capacity both to contribute these to others and to enjoy them oneself. Development of a positive self-image, a healthy sense of self-worth, is fundamental to much of the best of peace education at the early childhood and elementary grade levels.

The capacity for concern arises within a person's social development and hence primarily involves the communal sphere, where interpersonal relations develop in conjunction with a sense of self as member of a community and of other social groups—from family to nation, ethnic group, or religion—and ultimately as a part of the human species. It is in this sphere that the Leaven program focuses on education about the social and political issues that learners experience directly in their daily lives. This is also the arena in which specific skills and techniques—such as evaluative and critical skills and information-gathering abilities—are acquired and developed as the self becomes citizen.

The capacity for commitment encompasses the sphere that Leaven refers to as the "structural level" and Washburn and Gribbon speak of as the "global transpersonal." It requires the learner to have a functional appreciation for abstractions of social reality and its constituent elements, such as economic structures. Commitment calls for an ability to think of people whom we do not know directly—people from other cultures, other parts of the world, other times of history—as human beings. Also necessary are the intentional development of empathy for human conditions that learners themselves have not experienced, as well as the analytic capacity to understand the interrelational and structural causes for conditions that require empathy strong enough to lead to action.

A good deal of peace education today is directed toward these purposes, although in my opinion, not enough of it provides experience with structural analysis or with disciplined inquiry into alternative social structures. There is also a wide variety of programs designed to develop the sense of agency, or what many social educators refer to as a sense of "political efficacy." Political efficacy is recognized as a condition or attitude that can be developed through education. Having a sense of political efficacy is regarded as an attribute of maturity. Here is a case in which a major goal of peace education—that of guiding people toward intellectual and social maturity—is also an accepted goal of education in general, with the difference that peace education would transpose the sense of political efficacy into reconstruction as well as participation. Since the sphere of commitment is developmentally most important for promoting the actions and behaviors that can produce transformation, it is heartening to be able to identify specific curricula and practices already in place that are currently contributing to the development of a global, transpersonal capacity for commitment.

The Washburn-Gribbon approach is more developmental and is focused on human experience. They describe their three spheres as the *personal* ("living from the center") the *interpersonal* ("living in community"), and the *transpersonal* ("living as co-creators"). They give us invaluable insights into both the personal and the social developmental processes, aspects of which I have described in the sphere of cohesion. The Leaven approach is more structural and analytic, and, as pointed out in the curriculum guide, provides a useful way of introducing structural analysis into the secondary classroom. Both approaches are based on a concept of education that I would categorize as process learning. Recognizing that learners move in and out of developmental spheres during the process of maturation, they deal with these realities rather than imposing the sequential, hierarchical patterns typical of education in general. Learning is thus seen as an organic, flowing phenomenon. These approaches, as well as a variety of specific curricula I have seen, convince me that these concepts of quality and sphere have particular, readily identified, concrete applications to peace education, so that the transformational process learning that I advocate is not beyond the reach of any teacher.

Emerging Opportunities: Convergence of the Institutional and the Transformational

With the establishment of degree programs in peace studies in many colleges and universities, the introduction of nuclear age education and peace education into literally hundreds of schools, and the appearance of numerous books and articles on peace education, the climate is opportune for peace education to emerge as an important influence toward significant change in all educational practice. The legitimation of the field, with the establishment of the U.S. Institute for Peace and the University for Peace, indicates that the struggle for the recognition of this field of knowledge has been productive. It has provided the institutional and academic bases for a new stage of the struggle to gain recognition for peace education as necessary and practical. I sincerely hope that these institutions will flourish and that they will move beyond the substantive task to the transformational, becoming academic models for transcending the instrumentalism that has so impeded the larger struggle for peace.

Researchers, scholars, and educators have begun to address seriously the issues of the content and methodology of peace studies and peace education. I urge them now to undertake an exploration and discourse on the full nature of the transformation they seek and the qualities of an effective education for peace and global transformation. For I am convinced that only through such discourse can peace educators contribute to halting what Einstein called the "drift toward unparalleled catastrophe." I am equally convinced that we can and will make that contribution.

APPENDIX

REFERENCES

INDEX

ABOUT THE AUTHOR

Significant Works in the Development of the Pedagogy of Peace

The reflections in this volume represent a particular, and admittedly sub-jective, view of the development, substance, and purposes of peace edu-cation. Other peace educators of long experience would doubtless offer different interpretations. Much of what appears here results from years of discourse with colleagues — discourse through which we articulated strong agreement and significant differences — yet the exchanges were, for me, the kind of conversation I have asserted to be an essential element of process learning for transformational peace education. Although my own views are, I recognize, to some degree idiosyncratic, I believe all of us involved in this discourse have learned a great deal from each other. My own experience has provided me with the much-savored opportunity to participate in exchanges with the "pioneers." But much of the discourse, for me, has also been in the questions I brought to and the reflections inspired by reading in the field. Unfortunately the body of literature on peace education (distinct from peace studies, peace research, and all the components of global education, or what I refer to here as the pedagogy of peace, intentionally undertaken learning processes to develop peace-making capacities) is still limited enough to be manageable.

In this annotated bibliography I offer my own assessments of the works that I recommend to those seeking to learn more of the purposes and substance which have infused the contemporary international and transnational peace education movements. The list is, of course, selec-tive; however, it includes selections from both peace studies and peace education. Annotations of curricula and handbooks are to be found in the companion volume, *Educating for Global Responsibility: Teacher-Designed Curricula for Peace Education, K–12* (Teachers College Press, 1988).

These annotations constitute an attempt to pull together and describe some of the current scattered sources on the theory of peace education, a number of them internationally recognized as the foundations of the theory and pedagogy of the contemporary peace education movement, and all of them significant in my own thinking about the field. Over the past two decades journal articles, some of considerable theoretical significance, have sporadically appeared. Most American articles, however, have consisted of practical lesson plans and program descriptions or of arguments urging the need for peace or nuclear education. There has been no clearly definable conceptual or theoretical trend in the American professional literature on peace education until the recent spurt of articles on education relating to nuclear war and nuclear weapons. These, however, have tended to be more related to rationale and approaches than to theory or definition. Most of the work of this latter nature has been based on a particular philosophic or theological approach and directed toward education at the tertiary level. But, even there, the material on pedagogy per se is limited. Probably the most significant work in this area is to be found in the publications of organizations and institutions such as the Consortium on Peace Research, Education and Development (COPRED,) the World Policy Institute, the Institute for Peace and Justice, and the Justice and Peace Education Council, and recently some contributions from Educators for Social Responsibility.

In the area of nuclear weapons education even the most significant publications, the special issues of the nation's most prestigious educational journals (*Phi Delta Kappan, Teachers College Record*, and *Harvard Educational Review*), have given little space to conceptual and theoretical aspects of the pedagogy of peace.

The only consistently systematic literature on the subject has come from the international network of educators associated with the world's peace research community, mainly from UNESCO (of special note are the 1974 Recommendation concerning Education for International Understanding, Cooperation and Peace and Education relating to Human Rights and Fundamental Freedoms and the Final Document of the World Congress on Disarmament Education) and the International Peace Research Association (the IPRA Peace Education Commission is probably the most significant source). The major international periodicals that have published with some regularity on the subject have been, for the most part, peace-related journals (*Bulletin of Peace Proposals, Prospects, Gandhi Marg*, and the *Journal of Peace Studies*). These journals have also published special issues on peace education. (Only those containing theoretical material are included here.)

The same sources have produced the relatively few books on the subject, these tending to be mainly collections of previously published or specially commissioned articles by a variety of authors. The most significant source of such volumes is UNESCO (*Disarmament Education*) and individual peace educators (Haavelsrud, Sloan, Wulf). Many of these are included in this bibliography.

What follows here is an internationally derived, selected listing of sources, annotated so as to indicate the central themes and educational issues treated in the relevant works, and also to provide peace educators with an overview of the literature that reflects the theoretical and conceptual development of the field over the past two decades. The listing contains only secular sources that are substantively designated as concerned with peace education by the authors and/or publishers. Literature in the broader fields of international or global education or multicultural or development education are not included. Neither are there included here listings of works in the field that are from religious or denominational sources. The religious peace education movement and its materials are to be the subject of a subsequent work.

There are three categories of listings. The first are descriptions of landmark issues of professional journals. (A more comprehensive list of special issues on peace education is available from the Peace Education Program, Box 171, Teachers College, Columbia University, New York, NY 10027.) The second comprises a list of the major books, pamphlets, and individual publications on theory and methodology. The third is a list of peace research journals that reflect the conceptual development of the research field. Although some of these sources may be out of print, all should be available in university libraries.

Only English-language sources have been included. The paucity of listing is due in large part to the fact that although peace educators from all world areas publish in English, much of the significant theoretical work is in other languages. Particularly important are the untranslated works of Dutch, German, and Scandinavian peace educators. Fortunately, the leading, internationally known peace educators from these countries are represented in these annotations.

An asterisk at the end of a journal issue listing indicates that ordering information can be found in the section, "Sources on the Substance of Peace Research," at the end of this appendix.

Journals

Bulletin of the Atomic Scientists, Vol. 40, No. 10, December 1984. "Special Section: Nuclear War: A Teaching Guide," edited by Dick Ringler (also available separately from the *Bulletin* issue). Order from Educational Foundation for Nuclear Science, 5801 S. Kenwood, Chicago IL 60637.

Although there is only one article directed to education and teachers at the precollegiate levels (Alexander & Wagner), this educational supplement provides a short but comprehensive overview of nuclear education as it is presented at the university level, both graduate and undergraduate. It contains articles describing programs in nearly all the major disciplines as well as interdisciplinary, institutionwide, and interinstitutional programs, and offers resource listings. In these latter sections it does not distinguish clearly between nuclear education and peace studies. By far the best overall university resource listed is the fourth edition of the *Guide to Peace and World Order* studies, published by the World Policy Institute (see book annotations).

Bulletin of Peace Proposals, Vol. 5, No. 3, 1974. International Peace Research Institute, Oslo.*

One of the earliest efforts of a scholarly journal to focus on peace education, this issue contains only three original articles on peace education. However, there are abstracts and résumés of nineteen other articles and papers written between 1972 and 1974. These abstracts provide a really useful sample of both the substantive and methodological issues of peace education that were the basis of the research and discourse in the field in the seventies and of the ideas of the scholars and educators who were contributing to it. It provides descriptions of a wide range of approaches, from international understanding to conscientization, and offers the perspectives of ten different countries.

Of the original articles, contemporary peace educators will find especially interesting Robin Richardson's (U.K.) analysis of the field as influenced by three "voices," which he designates as "conservative, liberal and radical."

Bulletin of Peace Proposals, Vol. 10, No. 4, 1979. "Special Issue on Peace Education," edited by Burns Weston.*

This issue of the bulletin is an excellent example of the development of an authentic global stage of the peace education movement. Its thirteen articles from ten countries reflect the growing interest in perspectives from the Third World that began to enter the field in the early seventies, as well as the concern with the structural issues related to poverty in the developing countries. Two articles also forecast the emergence of the disarmament education approach. Several are concerned with educational methodology and the notion that the pedagogical means used in peace education must be consistent with the political ends.

Bulletin of Peace Proposals, Vol. 15, No. 2, 1984.*
   This, the most recent special peace education issue of the bulletin, is
notable for several reasons. Two articles (Young, and Al-Rubaiy et
al.) reflect a growing consciousness of the evolution of the field and
its sense of its own history. The issue shows, too, an acknowledge-
ment of the nature of the changing biases that have influenced peace
education, and it confronts the neutrality issue (Burns & Aspelagh).
It also reflects the continuation of a number of tensions within the
field and the introduction of new ones, most notably those that
attend to questions that feminist scholarship has begun to raise
about peace education and peace research (Brock-Utne). The issue
contains ten original articles by authors from ten countries.

Harvard Educational Review, Vol. 54, No. 3, August 1984. Special issue:
"Education and the Threat of Nuclear War." Available from *Harvard
Educational Review*, Longfellow Hall, 13 Appian Way, Cambridge, MA
02138.
   This issue of *HER* should be used as a companion to the journal's
special issue on international education. The focus is on negative
peace in the specific sense of the avoidance of nuclear war. It is a
good mix of theoretical (though not curriculum-theory) ideas about
the meaning and threat of nuclear weapons and "nuclearism, the
impact of the weapons on our culture" and practical approaches to
teaching and education. The interview with Lewis Thomas is extremely important. I recommend that it be read by all peace educators. It assesses the meaning of nuclear weapons to the present stage
of human development.

Harvard Educational Review, Vol. 55, No. 1, 1985. Special issue: "International Education: Perspectives, Experiences and Visions in an Interdependent World."
   On a number of counts this special issue is more consistent with a
comprehensive approach to peace education than *HER*'s earlier special issue on "Education and the Threat of Nuclear War." It takes a
critical stance, is conceived and executed from a global perspective,
and is based on a set of normative assertions, each article clearly
articulating a value or set of values as necessary to the purposes and
approaches of international education. In these respects it is a significant exception to mainstream international education and more
closely akin to peace education, which has been the most critical
wing of the field over the past few decades.
   As pointed out in Munir J. Fasheh's review of a recent volume

on international education published by the American Council on Education, the mainstream of the field appears to avoid the relevant, crucial global issues. This special issue, on the other hand, directly confronts them and, as Fasheh asserts the field should, makes them the central concern of the enterprise.

The volume is global in content as well as perspectives, with contributions from or about Brazil, El Salvador, Poland, Tanzania, and South Africa. One of the most significant articles, in terms of an approach consistent with comprehensive peace education, is that on development education by Joseph Short (pp. 32–44). Short clearly outlines some of the value concerns raised by study of the problems of development and asserts, "Such questions raise the likelihood that values clarification is not enough and that a fundamental change in values is undoubtedly at issue" (p. 39). His assertion is totally consistent with a fundamental assumption of most peace education, particularly those forms that focus on positive peace, social justice, and development. As I have noted in Chapter 1, this expression of the concerns of development educators comprises a list identical with those of peace educators.

> Development educators are seized by the urgency of the educational tasks that are posed by rapid change, pervasive violence, and human suffering within an outmoded and failing interstate system. They are worried that slow-moving educational systems will not adapt quickly enough. (p. 35)

The concept of positive peace calls upon peace education to confront the problem of racism. Ernest F. Duhe's article on racism and education in South Africa is very helpful on this issue, since it clearly defines three forms of racism and their origins in the European roots we share with South Africa.

Another particularly significant article is that on the Polish "Flying University" by Hanna Buczynka-Garewicz. We are reminded of the crucial role education can play in the struggle for the preservation of positive human values in this account of the inspiration and leadership that educators have provided under various oppressive phases of Polish history. Peace educators who find that their own efforts are not always without risk should find support in her observation,

> Because of this danger, a pattern of the courageous teacher was born. Courage is now understood as an essential virtue in a teacher. . . . All involvement in the educational process gained a particular moral approval. (p. 26)

The History and Social Science Teacher, Vol. 20, Nos. 3–4, Spring 1985. "Special Feature: Peace Education."

This double issue of a Canadian "journal of comment and criticism on social education" was jointly edited by Terry Carson and Barbara Roberts, two well-known, very active Canadian peace educators. It contains ten articles by Canadian, American, and Dutch peace educators who address issues related to the rationale for and the theory of peace education.

Although most of the articles focus on nuclear education, in his opening essay Terry Carson broadens the definition and concerns of peace education into the realm of positive peace:

> Our own preoccupation with the nuclear issue can also blind us to the more mundane forms of oppression suffered by others. Linking peace with justice, however, provides a basis for the development of positive conceptions of peace. (p. 9)

These positive conceptions account, no doubt, for the inclusion of Barbara Roberts and David Millar's article on violence against women, "A Peaceful World for Women: Peace Education Taking Gender into Account." It also reflects recent developments in the field, analyzing the linkages between sexist oppression and militarism and war.

Concepts of positive peace are also central to "Peace Education as Alternating Between the Person and the Structures," by the Dutch peace educators Lennart Vriens and Robert Aspelagh. This is an extremely important article, which outlines the fundamental theoretical bases of contemporary European peace education and offers a new theoretical formulation. It is essential reading for those wanting a firm theoretical grounding in the field and/or a global perspective.

This piece is somewhat of a contrast to the standard North American view presented by Walt Werner in "Conception of Peace Education." He notes that "There simply is little consensus on what peace education should entail" (p. 29). His piece, however, deals only with differing foci on nuclear education.

For subscription information, write to the journal at 16 Overlea Blvd., Toronto, Ont. MH4 1A6, Canada.

International Review of Education, Vol. 29, No. 3, 1983. Special issue: "The Debate on Education for Peace," edited by Magnus Haavelsrud and Johan Galtung.

The fifteen articles in this international collection are by authors from eleven countries, mainly European, two from eastern Europe, one from India, and one from Latin America. The one North American author (Marks) writes more from a global and/or European perspective (probably a consequence of years in the international movement with UNESCO). Thus, this journal may be the best single source on the conceptualizations, problems, and goals of peace education in the European setting. Emphasis is on positive peace. There is more attention to analytic and ideological questions than one finds in the American literature. However, the context of the analysis is peace education in the schools, so these essays provide American educators with a sound theoretical base and will acquaint them with the conceptual thinking of some of the major pioneers in the field, including one of the founders of peace research, the Norwegian scholar Johan Galtung. In the United States, this issue may be ordered from: Martinus Nyhoff Publishers, c/o Kenner Boston, Inc., 190 Old Derby Street, Hingham, MA 02043.

Peace and Change, A Journal of Peace Research, Vol. 10, No. 2, 19SN 0149-0508, Summer 1984. Special issue: "Peace Education for the Nuclear Age," edited by Mary E. Finn.*

This special issue of the journal of two peace research associations, the Consortium on Peace Research, Education and Development (COPRED) and the Committee on Peace Research in History (CPRH) contains eleven articles, by ten North Americans and one Israeli, organized into three sections.

The first section consists of a set of conference papers entitled "Conflict Resolution: Education Implications for the Nuclear Age." The focus of all save one article is far more on conflict than on the particular questions of the nuclear age. In her introduction Finn emphasizes the heuristic possibilities provided by the links and parallels between international education and peace education that help to globalize the discussion. There is, however, little or no discussion of the nature of the nuclear age and the unique issues it raises. Yet all the articles are substantively useful, and Barbara Stanford's "Thinking Beyond the Limits" should be required reading for peace educators, particularly any of those who espouse global transformation as the goal and framework for peace education. In what may well be seven of the most significant pages yet written in the field, she offers a comprehensive, succinct, and simple description of how we think about the world, how we came to think that way, and other potentially transformative modes of thinking about the human enterprise.

The second section, although it contains one piece on the lack of coverage of nuclear weapons and war in textbooks (Fleming), also fails to confront the fundamental philosophical and epistemological issues of the nuclear age. Nonetheless the materials on attitudes and values (Eckhardt) and methodology (Hazleton & Frey) provide useful background. Olivia Frey's "Pedagogy of Peace" is an excellent argument for the responsibility of peace educators to use methods that are consistent with the goals of reducing violence. The methods, she asserts, must be student-centered and require sensitivity to the thinking styles and developmental levels of the students. Mary Finn, in her article "Peace Education and Teacher Education," suggests "global interdependence" and "violent conflict" as conceptual categories for the review and assessment of peace education. (Only the latter category fits the criteria set forth in this volume.) Using these categories, she defines the related curricular areas of "global perspectives education" and "nuclear war education" and reviews some subcategories under each area before offering some reflections on learning objectives and teaching capabilities. She also reviews present programs in teacher education.

The third section, edited by Robert Ginsberg, is most useful for those educators seeking conceptual and definitional clarity. It contains the reflections of two philosophers (Cox and Kirkpatrick) and the values and constituent characteristics of peace.

I can highly recommend this collection of articles on peace education. It is the most significant contribution to the field in the United States since the advent of nuclear education.

Peace Research Reviews, Vol. 4, No. 1, March 1982.

This number of *PRR* contains the five prize-winning essays in the Wallach Awards Competition on the abolition of war and the requirements of peace. These essays are outstanding visions of the nature of peace and how to achieve it. They provide a conceptual background on the major ideas American scholars have proposed regarding the structural requirements of peace and the political strategies and processes necessary to build the structures. They are definitely something with which peace educators should be familiar and are quite readable enough to assign to senior high school students. What follows here are the descriptions of the articles printed as abstracts by the editors of *PRR*.

Gene Sharp's "Making the Abolition of War a Realistic Goal" is a persuasive and stimulating essay on the application of non-military, civilian based defense in contemporary politics. Historically, there have been many instances in which nonviolent resistance has been successful. (p. 2)

Homer Jack's "The New Abolition" catches the spirit of the Wallach Awards in its clear, urgent, unhesitating call for a new movement as strong and as fervent as the original movement that resulted in the successful abolition of slavery. "This New Abolitionism against a new form of slavery," says Dr. Jack, "is based on this single proposition: the development, production, stockpiling, threat to use, and the use of nuclear weapons by any nation or any group of individuals or nations is a crime against humanity." (p. 24)

John Somerville's "Philosophy of Peace Today: Preventive Eschatology" is a disturbing essay that reintroduces a long-forgotten philosophical discipline — the study of the end of the human world. The notion of preventive eschatology rests on the premise that known facts are not yet believed by the public. The problem, says Somerville, is educational: when documented facts are sufficiently believed, people will take political action. "Never did so much depend upon believing so little of what is already known." (p. 40)

Beverly Woodwards's "The Abolition of War," her Wallach essay, concludes with an invitation to moral reflection and action: "The problem of how to abolish war does not confront us exactly with an intellectual puzzle, although the intellect may assist in its solution. The problem we confront is fundamentally a problem that regards human will and human action. And although it is not usually put in these terms, it is a problem that regards human dignity. Humankind will have little claim to dignity, if we fail to undertake a concerted struggle against the war system and all that it entails and portends for our species." (p. 50)

Donald Keys' "The Abolition of War: Neglected Aspects" discusses psychological and attitudinal factors behind rising global militarism, the "hidden motors" that relentlessly drive the arms race. (p. 72)

Educators will also find useful for purposes of imaging a warless world and/or developing scenarios of the achievement of peace, the essays that appeared in the *Christian Science Monitor* in April 1985. Also recommended are studies of proposals for international peacekeeping, such as *World Peace Through World Law* (Cambridge, MA: Harvard University Press, 1958) and the United Nations peacekeeping efforts.

ReSearch, The Forum Humanum Journal, Vol. 1, No. 2, 1984.
This special issue (available from Pergamon Press, Maxwell House, Elmsford, NY 10523) is devoted to peace education and peace movements, treating the latter, as well, as learning experiences. American peace educators searching for definitions will find interesting an article on the notions of peace in modern Western philosophy (Falliero). Secondary educators will find a helpful analy-

sis of the potential for empowerment that young people are finding in the peace movement (Cela). Of interest to all concerned with the human future and universal or global perspectives in peace are two articles by the late founder of the Club of Rome and Forum Humanum, Aurelio Peccei. One article deals explicitly with education and its special responsibility in the confrontation of the negative factors that constitute the major human problems. The other, the posthumously published "Agenda for the End of the Century" sets forth a set of global goals, the achievement of which could constitute a peaceful and just world order. From our perspective, the most interesting point made here is the assertion that the "concept of nonviolence must become one of our basic cultural values" (p. 97).

Social Education, The Official Journal of the National Council for the Social Studies, Vol. 47, No. 7, November/December 1983. Special issue: "Nuclear Weapons: Concepts, Issues and Controversies," edited by Betty Reardon, John A. Scott, and Samuel Totten.

This special issue of the major journal for social educators provides a variety of resources for nuclear education, as well as useful background on the political climate in which it emerged. It is extremely important for peace educators to be well informed about the controversies that surround issues of war and peace and efforts to educate about them. Indeed, since the appearance of this special issue, which deals with the attack on the National Education Association for the publication of *Choices*, there have been continual assaults on various elements essential to peace education, including values analysis and curricula on the arms race.

Like the publications of Educators for Social Responsibility and the National Education Association (all annotated in this bibliography), this issue provides solid arguments for nuclear education as well as an overview of the charges against it. Moreover, it provides a sound pedagogical rationale and some specific practical tools. I especially advise peace educators to review the conceptual framework offered (Jacobson, Reardon, Sloan), since it comes from the same perspectives and pedagogical assumptions as inform the approach advocated in this book.

Teachers College Record, Vol. 84, No. 1, Fall 1982. Special issue: "Education for Peace and Disarmament: Toward a Living World," edited by Douglas Sloan.

This special issue of one of the most respected American journals of education was the first of the major special issues on education and the nuclear arms race. It has a distinct point of view that places peace education squarely at the center of the struggle for survival and meaning in the twentieth century. The major assertion of the editor who conceived and planned the issue is that "the primary task of education for peace is . . . to reveal and tap the reality of those energies and impulses that make possible the full human capacity for a meaningful and life-enhancing existence" (p. 1).

The articles range over a series of substantive peace issues that the editor describes as essential concerns for peace education: reversing the arms race, nonviolent defense options, nuclear freeze and nonintervention, concerns for teaching, philosophical dimensions, activism, the Peace Academy (now the U.S. Peace Institute), a critique of the peace movement, and civil defense.

It also departs from most other American journals' special issues on the topic in that it includes articles from abroad and some scenarios that can actually be used as teaching material. One very special feature is the last article ever written by Rene Dubos, "Education for the Celebration of Life and Optimism Despite It All." There is no stronger rationale for peace education than Dubos's last message.

Books, Pamphlets, and Monographs

Alexander, Susan. *Why Nuclear Education: A Sourcebook for Educators and Parents*. Cambridge, MA: Educators for Social Responsibility, 1984. 111 pp.

This sourcebook contains five sections that cover rationale for nuclear education; research concerning the psychological effects of the nuclear threat on children; a number of articles supporting the cause of nuclear education; the texts of resolutions of professional organizations and letters of advocacy; a section on materials, briefly annotated for the classroom teacher; and the entire special section on teaching about nuclear weapons from the December 1984 *Bulletin of the Atomic Scientists*. The publication is weakest on actual curricula and strongest on statements of rationale and the description and defense of critical-thinking approaches to nuclear education. It does offer some very useful criteria for the selection of curricula for teaching about nuclear weapons.

Becker, James N. *Teaching About Nuclear Disarmament*. Bloomington, Ind.: Phi Delta Kappa Educational Foundation, 1985. 37 pp.

This pamphlet (available from Phi Delta Kappa, Eighth and Union, Box 789, Bloomington, IN 47402) is very useful for placing nuclear education in both historical and contemporary context. Becker provides a brief overview of peace movements and peace education from World War I to the present. He defines some of the issues raised as a result of introducing questions of peace and nuclear disarmament into public education. The booklet also provides a basic bibliography for educators, an annotated list of curricular materials, and a list of resource organizations.

Brock-Utne, Birgit. *Educating for Peace: A Feminist Perspective*. New York: Pergamon Press, 1985. 164 pp.

Although the purpose of this book is the setting forth of a feminist theory of the pedagogy of peace, it is nonetheless as clear and comprehensive a definitional work as is to be found in the entire field. Brock-Utne makes a strong case that a feminist perspective may well be the basis for the overarching, holistic approach many educators have called for as the only appropriate framework for peace education.

The book is very well constructed, so as to provide a conceptual overview of the cultural environment that is both the arena and the subject of peace education. The author offers a sharp diagnostic critique of both the socialization imposed by the culture and the instruction offered by the schools. In so doing, she shows the social realities that help to perpetrate war and also clearly shows the outline of what is to be changed if we are to educate for peace.

Especially helpful is the fact that she defines the terms and stipulates her assumptions, the most fundamental of which is the crucial need for significant changes in our values and in the way we think. She raises the essential question for education in our time: "How do we begin to rethink? And how do we teach the whole society to re-educate itself?" (p. 72). "This," she says, "is the task peace education has set for itself. . . . *peace education* [is] *the social process through which peace . . . is achieved.*"

She defines peace mainly in terms of human equality and non-violence and then proceeds to explore how the current educational system and socialization processes discourage these values in boys while encouraging them in girls. Throughout she offers concrete examples of her diagnosis of the problems and her prescriptions for overcoming them.

This book is recommended as a good conceptual overview of the field of peace education and the problems it must confront.

Carpenter, Susan. *A Repertoire of Peacemaking Skills*. Boulder, CO: Consortium on Peace Research Education and Development, 1977. 60 pp.

This handbook is still the best single resource for the development of learning objectives in the area of positive peace. Starting from the premise that structural violence is as dangerous a threat to peace as is the physical violence of war, the *Repertoire* sees the task of education as preparing students to be peacemakers. It is an action- and agent-oriented approach to peace education, which asserts that we need to teach how to engage in the behaviors that make peace. It clearly indicates that peace-making can be learned and that educators can learn to teach it.

It is a sound work, not only well grounded theoretically and straightforward about its assumptions; it is also eminently practical. It lists skills, provides methods for their development, and offers sample cases to demonstrate when and how they might be applied.

If a peace educator can obtain only one resource, this should be the one.

Carson, Terry, ed. *Dimensions and Practice of Peace Education*. Edmonton: University of Alberta, Department of Secondary Education, 1985.

This volume was compiled as a set of course readings for the intensive short course that preceded the International Institute on Peace Education held at the University of Alberta in July of 1985.

It brings together selections from several of the journals and volumes that are annotated in this bibliography. It serves as a concise introduction to the present state of the art in the theory of and approaches to peace education. The collection is international and recent, with the exception of a 1974 piece by Johan Galtung and a 1979 editorial from the *Bulletin of Peace Proposals*. The materials are organized into five sections; an introduction, followed by sections on "Positive and Negative Conceptions of Peace," "Militarism and Non-Violent Action," "Critical Context of Peace Education in Classrooms Situations," and "Problems of Pedagogy in Peace Education."

It leans heavily toward the structural approach, with little emphasis on issues of negative peace. There are no discussion questions or proposed framework for analyzing the essays, nor is there any specified criteria for their selection. All of this collateral material was provided in class discussion. However, even for those who were not participants, the readings constitute a good introductory collection.

Genser, Lillian, ed. 1976. *Understanding and Responding to Violence in Young Children*. Detroit: Wayne State University, Center for Teaching About Peace and War, 1976. 51 pp.

Although this booklet (available from the Center for Peace and Conflict Studies, 5229 Cass Avenue, Detroit, MI 48202) was published over a decade ago, it is still a unique (unfortunately) and essential resource for peace education. It is one of the few publications for American educators that attempts to analyze a significant aspect of the core peace problem, violence. It is especially helpful to American peace educators because it illuminates the cultural context in which we do our work, making evident that our task is far greater than just developing curricula and teaching methods. We must see our work in peace education as integral to fulfilling the need for a profound cultural change. The need for such a change is well documented by the essays that comprise the booklet.

Esther D. Callard points out that children are not born violent. Some are made to become violent by the way society perceives and responds, interpreting children's actions as violent, beginning with the "kicking" of the unborn infant. She explores these issues in the context of the responsibilities of teachers confronted by the violent behavior of children and by the problems of children living in conditions of violence.

William Wattenberg, focusing on elementary school children, explores questions of how the socialization process might be changed so as to reduce violent behavior in young children. He finds the major antidote in an education that offers the child fun and warmth in lieu of hate and violence.

Mel Ravitz establishes some links between various forms of social violence and militarism. Among other prescriptive assertions, he states,

> To reduce violence in America we will have to change the way we relate to our children at home and in school. We'll have to provide them with better nonviolent models than we have and begin to encourage different priorities on television and in our everyday lives . . .
>
> To reduce violence in America will require us to remake the American experience and the American culture (p. 71).

A workshop report by Wilfred Innerd generated an agenda of questions to be addressed by all peace educators.

Haavelsrud, Magnus, ed. *Approaching Disarmament Education*. Guildford, England: Westbury House, 1981.
This collection results largely from work done in preparation for or follow-up of UNESCO's World Conference on Disarmament Education, held in Paris in 1980. The volume was published in association with the Peace Education Commission of the International Peace

Research Association, whose members are among the main contributors. It covers much that is relevant to the relationships among the political problems of disarmament, disarmament research, and disarmament education. Although there are attempts to specifically and conceptually clarify the role of disarmament education within education for peace, the tensions and debates over the issues are apparent (e.g., Aspelagh & Wiese, "Recent discussions on disarmament education," pp. 1–7). It demonstrates the significant role that UNESCO has played in the conceptual development of all fields of peace education, as well as the very distinct approaches and stances to be found in each area of the world regarding disarmament education and education for peace.

Haavelsrud, Magnus, ed. *Education for Peace: Reflection and Action* (Proceedings of the First World Conference of the World Council for Curriculum and Instruction, University of Keele, UK, September 1974). Surrey, England: International Peace Commission and Technology Press, 1975.

Contains 30 articles from 20 countries dealing with the substantive and methodological aspects of peace education, from early childhood to university level and out of school. Contributors analyze, from their cultural viewpoint, basic questions, such as: What is peace education? Why is it needed? How should it be done? Where is it needed most? The book results from the first World Conference on Education of the World Council for Curriculum and Instruction held at the University of Keele in September 1974. More than a set of proceedings, it is a collection of articles by leaders in both the practical realms of international conflict (i.e., the United Nations and the International Peace Academy) and pioneers in peace research and education (e.g., Galtung, Freire, and Adam Curle, the Founder of the Peace Studies Program at Bradford University). It is a good introduction to the practice of the field in many parts of the world in the early seventies and to some of the early theoretical work on pedagogy (e.g., Diaz, Haavelsrud, Richardson, and Ukita, all of whom have subsequently published quite widely in peace education).

Henderson, George, ed. *Education for Peace: Focus on Mankind.* Washington, DC: Association for Supervision and Curriculum Development, 1973.

"Who can live without hope?" This query from Sandberg's *The People, Yes*, quoted in the prefatory section of this collection of essays, captures the spirit of this volume. As the 1973 yearbook of the Association for Supervision and Curriculum Development, *Education for Peace: Focus on Mankind,* can indeed be considered a landmark work. It was the first publication of its kind in this era of peace education to be issued from an "establishment" source. It is with some regret that I report that the essays that comprise the volume (like several of the curricula from the 1970s described in Reardon, 1988) are still relevant. In fact, the first, Thornton B. Monez's "Working for Peace: Implications for Education," continues to be a fundamental and essential conceptual introduction to violence as the core issue of peace education. Aubrey Haan's "Antecedents of Violence" connects the issue so clearly to all of our social institutions, including schools, that it is essential reading for American peace educators. It contains the now classic "Children and the Threat of Nuclear War," by Sibylle Escalona, and other pieces that also reflect the significance of the Vietnam experience to our society and to educators concerned with transforming it toward more peaceful ways. The preface and closing chapter by the editor reflect those elements that give rise to hope and place the work clearly within a framework of comprehensive peace education. No American peace education collection should be without this very small and very significant book.

Johnson, David M., ed. *Justice and Peace Education Models for Colleges and University Faculty.* Maryknoll, NY: Orbis Books, 1985.
This book is a collection of essays on peace and justice education by sixteen distinguished Catholic educators, describing approaches to the field within the various scholarly disciplines. Edited by David Johnson, associate executive director of the Association of Catholic Colleges and Universities, the volume recapitulates the history of the development of the field in Catholic institutions of higher education and describes model programs designed and implemented by individuals and teams of the faculties of some of those institutions. With a substantive introduction by Joseph Fahey, director of a pioneering peace studies program at Manhattan College, it provides both the why and the how of justice and peace education in Catholic academic settings.

Although it emanates from and is directed toward Catholic educators, the volume is primarily concerned with the disciplines and the educational process as such. The essays are organized into four sections, reflecting the academic categories under which peace studies are frequently organized: the humanities, the social sciences, the professional disciplines, and interdisciplinary courses. They manifest a clear demonstration that peace studies can be integrated into virtually the entire university curriculum.

An article that will be of special interest to the readers of this book is by Mildred Haipt, O.S.U., who contributed a curriculum that appears in the companion volume (no. 6). Sr. Haipt deals with the discipline of education and makes a strong case for the integration of peace and justice education into teacher education. She also presents several concrete models of how to do it (social analysis, problem posing, and concept infusion) and offers an excellent list of "Selected Readings for Faculty." This chapter is especially recommended for teacher educators.

Murray, Andrew M. *Peace and Conflict Studies as Applied Liberal Arts: A Theoretical Framework for Curriculum Development.* Huntingdon, Pa.: Published by the author, 1980.

This brief and useful introduction to a conflict studies approach to negative peace was written as a doctoral dissertation and was fairly widely distributed through the peace studies community by the Church of the Brethren and United Ministries in Education. It offers frameworks for analyzing processes of conflict and cooperation. Along with a good overview of the best research on the topics, it provides concrete suggestions as to how the concepts and knowledge produced by this research can be introduced into all the standard disciplines of the liberal arts.

Nuclear Arms Education in Secondary Schools. Muscatine, IA: The Stanley Foundation, 1985. 22 pp.

This booklet, sponsored by the National Council for the Social Studies, the Social Studies Development Center of Indiana University, and the Johnson Foundation, is an essential resource for all secondary school teachers involved in or considering teaching about nuclear weapons. Available from the Stanley Foundation (420 East Third St., Muscatine, IA 52761), it is the single most concise, conceptually sound, and thorough overview of content and issues in nuclear education currently available. Based upon the report of a conference of leading American social educators, the booklet includes guidelines for dealing with controversy, an outline of basic topics for study of the issues, and suggestions on rationale, goals, approaches, and evaluation. It clearly states the need to educate for the prevention of nuclear war but sets forth the parameters for that education in an objective, nonpartisan fashion, advocating legitimate inquiry. Teachers are urged to give thorough consideration to the following teaching guidelines offered in the booklet (p. 5):

> The issue must be
> 1. Presented in a way that is relevant to the students and to the subject or course being taught.
> 2. Appropriate to the age and maturity level of the students involved.
> 3. Regarded by the teaching profession as important.
> 4. Not disruptive to school or classroom discipline.
>
> Treatment of the issue must provide
> 1. Multiple perspectives on the topic.
> 2. Information, *not* politicization.
>
> Treatment of the issue must avoid
> 1. Exploiting emotional trauma.
> 2. Promoting feelings of alienation or despair.
> 3. Treating this issue from only one viewpoint.

O'Hare, Padraic, ed. *Education for Peace and Justice*. New York: Harper & Row, 1983.

Designed primarily to provide background and professional insights to the religious educator, this book offers important material on methods and objectives for all peace educators. All of the authors of the sixteen original articles are Roman Catholic, North American religious educators who bring together the Catholic social-doctrine tradition, which links social justice inextricably to peace, and a learner-centered approach to education for social change. There is a very strong emphasis on the asserted need for consistency between social ends and educational means. Although there is more theology than most outside the religious education field will find useful, there are very helpful applications of moral-development theory to teaching about justice and peace and an exploration of the relevance and relationship of the theories of John Dewey and Paulo Freire to peace education, which could well constitute required reading for all teachers in the field at all levels of formal education.

Reardon, Betty. *Militarization, Security and Peace Education*. Valley Forge, PA: United Ministries in Education, 1982. 93 pp.

This is a six-section study and discussion guide for adult education. It has also been used in teacher education courses as a basic introduction to the substance, approaches, and goals of peace education. It was designed to facilitate the introduction of peace education into elementary and secondary schools by informing the community and enlisting its support.

It defines the problems of war and injustice within the context of the militarization process evident in the arms race and its consequences to the real security of the human family in military, economic, and social terms. The emphasis is placed on human needs and the impediments to their fulfillment inherent in the war system. It takes an approach that integrates and relates positive and negative peace.

Militarization offers a general introduction to peace education by outlining the skills and values to be developed and specifies the broad set of learning objectives that are integral to comprehensive peace education.

Each section is followed by review and discussion questions to assist in the reflective process necessary to prepare for undertaking action on behalf of peace education. It lists and categorizes resources for deeper and more extensive study. Most significantly, it offers specific action strategies and a general plan for the introduction of peace education into the schools. It would make a good companion to this volume and the curriculum guide.

Saperstein, David. *Preventing the Nuclear Holocaust: A Jewish Response.* New York: United American Hebrew Congregation, 1983.

This excellent resource (available from Religious Action Center, 2027 Massachusetts Avenue N.W., Washington, DC 20036) will be invaluable to any educator taking a comparative religious approach to the study of war, the arms race, and/or nuclear weapons. It also comprises an excellent set of sources on nuclear issues. Although it emphasizes a Jewish perspective and Jewish concerns such as questions related to Israel and Soviet Jewry, it would prove a useful general resource for any educator interested in an overview collection of materials in nuclear weapons. In addition to a fine set of essays on the biblical, theological, and traditional Jewish teachings on war, it also offers reprints, original essays, and other resources on most major nuclear-weapons policy issues. It contains, as well, an extensive section on study and action suggestions. It is at a higher reading level than that of most secondary school students, but it is an excellent background resource for educators.

Stine, Esther, et al. *Education in a Global Age.* Public Education Policy Studies. Dallas: United Ministries in Education, 1983. 33 pp.

This brief monograph (available from United Ministries in Education Resource Center, 13756 Rolling Hills, Dallas, TX 75240) is one of the most significant of all sources on global education for the peace educator. It provides a useful descriptive narrative within a constructively critical framework. The framework, an explicitly value-based orientation to the field, raises issues related to the fundamental purposes and objectives of global education. The three critical values identified in this United Ministries in Education policy study, originally drafted by the Educational and Leadership Development staff of the Program Agency of the United Presbyterian Church USA, are justice, peace, and human rights. The issues presented in this monograph have also been raised by practitioners who are developing global education for the schools. I would suggest that the Stine paper be read jointly with two issues of *Social Education*, the issue of October 1986, "Special Section on Global Education," and that of November/December 1986, "Scope and Sequence," especially the article by Willard M. Kneip, the editor of the October special section. Although peace education is not the focus of these issues, they reflect the more normative and change-oriented approach that the field of global education appears to be developing.

Thomas, T. M., David Conrad, and Gertrude Langsam. *Global Images of Peace and Education: Transforming the War System*. Ann Arbor: Prakken, 1987.

One of the most recent collections of essays on war–peace issues and the challenge of these issues to contemporary education, this volume was sponsored by the Society for Educational Reconstruction. The contents, contributed by authors from universities throughout the United States, are divided into three main parts. The first, dealing with the conditions that call for transformation, "From a War System to Peace and Justice," is preceded by the editor's preface, "From A Warring World to a Peaceful Global Order," outlining the ethical bases of the volume and the normative purposes of its educational recommendations. Part II, "Education for Global Consciousness," offers a set of essays that describe teaching approaches and activities cast in an intentionally transformative mode. Part III, "Perspectives on World Community," is comprised of essays dealing with conceptual components of a transformative process of education.

Wien, Barbara, ed. *Peace and World Order Studies*. 4th ed. New York: World Policy Institute, 1984.

This, the fourth in the series of volumes begun with the publication of the Wehr and Washburn edition in 1976 (others were Weston, Schwenninger, & Shamis, 1978, and Feller, Schwenninger, & Singerman, 1981), is far more comprehensive that the preceding three. It covers nearly every discipline taught in higher education, including some of the newer ones, such as women's studies. The volume overflows with well-detailed syllabi, course outlines, and bibliographies. It is well organized for easy reference according to academic disciplines.

The introductory essay by Peter Dale Scott reflects much of the normative nature of the field and its growth in substantive and methodological sophistication. However, not all of the entries are of such a level of sophistication as to preclude their adaptation to senior high school. It is a rich resource for this purpose. For teachers at any level interested in bibliography and/or the state of the art in contemporary American peace studies, this is an essential resource. As this volume goes to press, a fifth edition is being compiled and edited under the sponsorship of the Peace and World Security Studies Project at Hampshire College, Amherst, MA.

Wilson, G. K. *A Global Peace Study Guide*. London: Housmans, 1982. 101 pp.

Although this guide does not offer much by way of rationale, theory, or methodology for peace education as these have been defined in this volume, it is an excellent resource for peace education. It is a kind of mini-encyclopedia of the terminology, theories, and historical development of peace research. It offers a rich array of conceptual definitions, historical and cultural roots of peace concepts, listings of other data sources, and a chronological bibliography of the study of peace. The bibliography alone is worth the purchase price. It must be stressed, though, that the booklet is more a reference work than a substantive one.

Wulf, Christoph, ed. *Handbook on Peace Education*. Oslo: International Peace Research Association, 1974.

This is an extremely significant volume, certainly the first of its kind produced in Europe and perhaps a world first. It resulted from an international conference entitled "Education for Peace and Social Justice," held at Bad Nauheim, Federal Republic of Germany, in November 1972, under the sponsorship of the International Peace Research Association, the Institute for World Order, and several German research associations. The featured speakers and main contributors to the volume were peace researchers from every part of the world — east, west, north, and south — providing for a global overview, if not so wide an ideological spectrum on the issues covered. The first section, on concepts, has little to do with learning process or pedagogy, but it does provide an excellent overview of some of the main issues that are still significant to the field and offers an expression of some of the tensions, still not totally resolved, that arose in the early efforts at cooperation between researchers and educators. The contributors were and are still among the leaders in the world community of peace researchers: Johan Galtung, Saul Mendlovitz, Elise Boulding, Kinhide Mushakoji (now vice rector of the United Nations University). The second section, on approaches, however, offers only two names that have remained familiar in the international peace education community, Nicklas and Osterman, whose work also appears in some of the journals annotated here. The third section, reporting on peace education as practiced in Europe and the United States (there is one contribution from Chile), reveals how the young academic field was still strongly rooted in the parent fields of international relations and international understanding and how little had yet been done to meet the specific pedagogical needs of preparation for peacemaking. Although weak with regard to learning process, this work is still conceptually very important. Because of this and its historical significance to the development of the field, it certainly should have a place in every serious collection on peace education.

Sources on the Substance of Peace Research

The content of peace education in the formal sector has been based largely on the information and theories formulated through peace research. Although peace educators, too, have contributed some significant insights to peace knowledge, without interaction and cooperation with researchers and peace-activities and peace-development practitioners, educators cannot, I think, develop a truly comprehensive approach to peace education.

To keep apprised of developments in research and formal study, peace educators are urged to read regularly one or more of the following journals, which are among the best known of the growing number of peace journals. This list was prepared by Debora St. Claire James, a graduate student in the Peace Education Program of Teachers College, Columbia University.

Alternatives. Quarterly, published by Butterworths, for the Centre for the Study of Developing Societies and the World Order Models Project, Guildford, England. Subscription inquiries should be addressed to: Quadrant Subscriptions Services Ltd., Oakfield House, Perrymount Road, Haywards Heath RH16 3DH, England.

This journal examines world order studies from a holistic, transformative perspective. Its articles focus on global issues concerning policy, North–South tensions, and peace and justice. *Alternatives* would be of interest to educators and researchers interested in examining the interconnections among global problems.

Bulletin of Peace Proposals. Quarterly, published by the International Peace Research Institute, Oslo, Norway. Subscription and back-issue inquiries should be addressed to Publications Expediting Inc., 200 Meacham Ave., Elmont NY 11003.

The *Bulletin of Peace Proposals* looks at contemporary international issues concerning peace and justice. The contributors, international peace researchers and educators, address alternatives and possibilities for a more peaceful future. In general, articles report on current research and problem analysis, which educators may find useful, but special issues focusing on peace education are of particular interest.

COPRED Peace Chronicle. Bimonthly, published by the Consortium on Peace Research, Education, and Development (COPRED). Subscription inquiries should be addressed to COPRED, c/o Center for Conflict Resolution, George Mason University, 4400 University Dr., Fairfax VA 22030.

This newsletter for COPRED members discusses business, activities, and reports from the various networks of COPRED. It includes a calendar of national and international conferences and a listing of recent publications concerning peace issues. This is an important newsletter for those wishing to keep up with current peace research, education, and action in the United States.

Disarmament. Quarterly, published by the United Nations Department of Disarmament Affairs. Subscription inquiries should be addressed to: Room DC2-853, United Nations, New York, NY 10017.

This journal covers UN conventions, initiatives, and resolutions concerning disarmament. The articles, contributed by UN ambassadors, counselors, and affiliates, address the role of the UN, relationships among countries, and development issues as they relate to disarmament. It would be of particular interest to educators interested in disarmament education.

International Peace Research (IPRA) Newsletter. Quarterly; subscription inquiries should be addressed to Clovis Brigagao, Secretary General, International Peace Research Association, Rup. Ipu 26, Bloco 2, Apto. 5, CEP 2281, Rio de Janeiro, R.J., Brazil.

This newsletter contains short articles regarding peace and conflict issues, but the bulk of the publication is devoted to news regarding the various IPRA commissions and reports from peace researchers around the world. It also includes a calendar of international peace conferences and seminars. This is an important guide for anyone who desires to be informed on the work of international peace educators and researchers.

International Peace Studies Newsletter. Quarterly, published by the Center for Peace Studies, University of Akron. Subscription inquiries should be addressed to Center for Peace Studies, University of Akron, Akron, OH 44325.

This newsletter features two or three articles concerning peace studies at the university level relevant to peace educators and peace students. The newsletter gives listings of programs on peace and international issues at other institutions and a brief calendar of upcoming conferences and events in the field.

Journal of Peace Research. Quarterly, published by the International Peace Research Institute, Oslo. Subscription and back-issue inquiries should be addressed to Publications Expediting, Inc., 200 Meacham Ave., Elmont, NY 11003.

This journal is analysis-oriented. It focuses on peace issues from a problematic and theoretical perspective. This highly academic journal tackles topical issues of current concern to international peace researchers.

Peace and Change. Quarterly, sponsored by the Committee on Peace Research in History and the Consortium on Peace Research Education and Devlopment (COPRED). Subscription and back-issue inquiries should be addressed to Center for Peaceful Change, Kent State University, Kent, OH 44242.

Peace and Change focuses on peace issues from an educational and historical perspective. Its viewpoint is mainly American. Its essays concerning historical analysis and the development of peace movements and peace education would be of particular interest to educators.

Peace Research: Canadian Journal of Peace Studies. Published three times a year by the Canadian Peace Research and Education Association (CPREA). Subscription inquiries should be addressed to Dr. M. V. Naidu, Professor of Political Science, Brandon University, Manitoba, Canada, R7A 6A9.

Peace Research, emphasizing Canadian issues, is also of interest to American peace scholars and researchers, because of its broad spectrum of articles concerning peace. A CPREA newsletter is enclosed in each issue.

Peace Research Abstracts. Monthly, published by Peace Research Institute-Dundas, 25 Dundana Avenue, Dundas, Ontario, Canada, L9H 4E5. This journal is a vast compilation of abstracts concerning a wide range of peace and conflict issues. The index is divided into ten major topics, which are subdivided into 350 subtopics. This extremely well-indexed journal is an important resource for anyone researching in the field of peace, conflict, and international studies.

References

Augros, R., & Stanciu, G. (1984). *The new story of science*. Chicago: Gateway Editions.

Beer, F. (1983). *Peace against war: The ecology of international violence*. San Francisco: W. H. Freeman.

Belenky, M., Clinchy, B., Goldberger, N., & Tarule, J. (1986). *Women's ways of knowing*. New York: Basic Books.

Boulding, E. (1976). *The underside of history: A view of women through time*. Boulder, CO: Westview Press.

Boulding, K. (1978). *Stable peace*. Beverly Hills: Sage.

Boulding, K. (1985, May). Learning by simplifying complexity. *United Nations University Newsletter, 8*(3), 5.

Brock-Utne, B. (1985). *Educating for peace, a feminist perspective*. New York: Pergamon Press.

Brookfield, S. (1986). Media, power and the development of media literacy: An adult educational interpretation. *Harvard Educational Review, 66*, 2.

Buergenthal, T., & Torney, J. (1976). *International human rights and international education*. Washington, DC: U.S. National Commission for UNESCO.

Carey, L., & Kanet, K. (1985). *Leaven*. Silver Springs, MD: Sisters of Mercy of the Union.

Carpenter, S. (1977). *Repertoire of peacemaking skills*. Boulder, CO: Consortium on Peace Research Education and Development.

Carson, T. (1985). Relating peace education and social studies in an age of insecurity. *History and Social Science Teacher, 20*(3-4), 8-10.

Childers, E. (1985). Presentation to Teachers College course on "The United Nations and Development." Teachers College, Columbia University, New York.

Diallo, D., & Reardon, B. (1981). The creation of a pedagogic institute of peace. In *Basic documents* (pp. 195-197). San José, Costa Rica: The Presidential Commission for the University for Peace.

Eisler, R., & Loye, D. Peace and feminist theory: New directions. *Bulletin of Peace Proposals, 17*(1), 95-99.

Feller, G., Schwenninger, S., & Singerman, D. (Eds.). (1981). *Peace and world order studies: A curriculum guide* (3rd ed.). New York: Institute for World Order.

Frank, J. (1968). *Sanity and survival*. New York: Vintage.

Freire, P. (1973). *The pedagogy of the oppressed*. New York: Herder & Herder.

Galtung, J. (1969). Violence and peace research. *Journal of Peace Research, 7*(3), n.p.

Giarini, O. (1985, May). The consequences of complexity in economics. *United Nations University Newsletter, 8*(3), 7.

Gilligan, C. (1982). *In a different voice.* Cambridge, MA: Harvard University Press.

Hunt, M., & Metcalf, L. (1955). *Teaching high school social studies.* New York: Harper & Row.

Jacobson, W. (1982). A generalized approach to societal problems. *Science Education, 66*(5), 699–708.

Jacobson, W. (1984, February). *Why nuclear education.* Paper presented at the Second Annual Nuclear Issues Conference, New York.

Jacobson, W., Reardon, B., & Sloan, D. (1983). A conceptual framework for teaching about nuclear weapons. *Social Education, 47*(7), 475–479.

Johansen, R. (1980). *The national interest and human interest: An analysis of U.S. foreign policy.* Princeton, NJ: Princeton University Press.

Johnson, D. (1985). *Justice and peace education models for college and university faculty.* Maryknoll, NY: Orbis Books.

Johnson, R., & Johnson, D. (Eds.). (1984). *Structuring cooperative learning: Lesson plans for teachers.* Minneapolis: Interaction Books.

Juniata consultation on the future of peace studies. (1986, December). *COPRED Peace Chronicle, 11*(6), 3–4.

Kniep, W. M. (1986, October). Defining global education by its content. *Social Education, 50*(6), 437–446.

Kohlberg, L. (1983). *Psychology of moral development.* New York: Harper & Row.

Laor, R. (1976). *A competency based program for cooperating teachers in modeling behaviors designated to assist pupils in developing helping and caring values.* Unpublished doctoral dissertation, Teachers College, Columbia University, New York.

McIntyre, M., Tobin, L., & Johns, H. (1976). *Peaceworld.* New York: Friendship Press.

Macy, J. R. (1983). *Despair and empowerment in a nuclear age.* New York: Random House.

Marks, S. (1983). Peace, development, and human rights education: The dilemma between the status quo and curriculum overload. *International Review of Education, 29*(3), 289–307.

Matriano, E., & Reardon, B. (1976, April). *A global community perspective on education for development.* Paper presented at Global Education Working Group, Chulalongkorn University, Bangkok, Thailand.

Mendlovitz, S. (Ed.). (1982). *Studies on a just world order.* Boulder, CO: Westview Press.

Mische, G., & Mische, P. (1977). *Toward a human world order.* New York: Paulist Press.

Muller, R. (n.d.). *A world core curriculum.* Unpublished manuscript, University for Peace, San José, Costa Rica.

Murray, A. (1980). *Peace and conflict studies*. Huntingdon, PA: Author.

O'Hare, B. (1983). *Education for justice and peace*. Maryknoll, NY: Orbis Books.

Oliver, D., & Shaver, J. (1974). *Teaching public issues in the high school* (2nd ed.). Logan: Utah State University Press.

Reardon, B. (1982). *Militarization, security, and peace education*. Valley Forge, PA: United Ministries in Education.

Reardon, B. (1983). Research agenda for a gender analysis of militarism and sexist repression. *International Peace Research Newsletter, 21*(2), 3-10.

Reardon, B. (1984, July). *The University for Peace: Curricular proposals and approaches*. Paper presented at the Triennial Conference of the International Association of University Presidents, Bangkok, Thailand.

Reardon, B. (1985). *Sexism and the war system*. New York: Teachers College Press.

Reardon, B. (1987). Civic responsibility to a world community. In T. Thomas et al. (Eds.), *Global images of peace* (pp. 253-263). Ann Arbor, MI: Prakken.

Reardon, B. (1988). *Educating for global responsibility: Teacher-designed curricula for peace education, K-12*. New York: Teachers College Press.

Reardon, B. (In press). Toward a paradigm of peace. In Linda R. Forcey (Ed.), *Thinking about peace: Interdisciplinary perspectives*. Greenwood, NY: Praeger.

Rifkin, J. (1985). *The declaration of a heretic*. Boston: Routledge & Kegan Paul.

Schell, J. (1982). *The fate of the earth*. New York: Alfred A. Knopf.

Sharp, G. (1974). *Politics of nonviolent action*. Boston: Porter Sargent.

Sivard, R. (1985). *World military and social expenditures*. Leesburg, VA: World Priorities.

Sloan, D. (1982). Toward an education for a living world. *Teachers College Record, 84*(1), 1-3.

Sloan, D. (1983). *Toward a recovery of wholeness*. New York: Teachers College Press.

Sloan, D. (1984). *Insight, imagination, and the emancipation of the modern mind*. Westport, CT: Greenwood.

Stanford, B. (1976). *Peacemaking: A guide to conflict resolution for individuals, groups and nations*. New York: Bantam Books.

Thorpe, G., & Reardon, B. (1971). Simulation and world order. *High School Journal, 55*(2), 53-62.

UNESCO. (1974). *Recommendation on education for international understanding, cooperation and peace, and education concerning human rights and fundamental freedoms*. Paris: UNESCO.

UNESCO. (1980a). *Final document of the World Congress on Disarmament Education*. Paris: UNESCO.

UNESCO. (1980b). *The status of and recommendations for disarmament education* (SS/80, Conf. 603). Paris: UNESCO.

University for Peace. (1985, January). *Memo on curriculum development*. Working document of the 1983 meeting of the Council of the University for Peace, San José, Costa Rica.

Vio Grossi, F. (1985, November). *Closing remarks*. Address delivered at the World Assembly on Adult Education, Buenos Aires, Argentina.

Walbek, N., & Weiss, T. (1974). *A world order framework for teaching international relations*. New York: Institute for World Order.

Washburn, P., & Gribbon, R. (1986). *Peace without division: Moving beyond congregational apathy and anger*. Washington, DC: Alban Institute.

Wehr, P., & Washburn, M. (1976). *Peace and world order systems teaching and research*. Beverly Hills: Sage.

Weston, B., Schwenninger, S., & Shamis, D. (1978). *Peace and world order studies*. New York: Institute for World Order.

Wien, B. (Ed.). (1984). *Peace and world order studies: A curriculum guide* (4th ed.). New York: World Policy Institute.

Index

About the Author

BETTY REARDON, director of the Peace Education Program of Teachers College, Columbia University, has been active for many years in the development of peace education. She was one of the founders of the Peace Education Commission of the International Peace Research Association and has done extensive consulting with various international and national organizations and educational institutions. Her writings on peace education, disarmament education, human rights, and women's issues have been widely published in the United States and abroad.